...nations around the world,
sharing with travellers a wealth of
experience and a passion for travel.

**Rely on Thomas Cook as your
travelling companion on your next trip
and benefit from our unique heritage.**

Thomas Cook **pocket** guides

VERONA

Written by Barbara Radcliffe Rogers
Updated by Jo-Ann Titmarsh

Published by Thomas Cook Publishing
A division of Thomas Cook Tour Operations Limited
Company registration No: 3772199 England
The Thomas Cook Business Park, 9 Coningsby Road
Peterborough PE3 8SB, United Kingdom
Email: books@thomascook.com, Tel: +44 (0)1733 416477
www.thomascookpublishing.com

Produced by The Content Works Ltd
Aston Court, Kingsmead Business Park, Frederick Place
High Wycombe, Bucks HP11 1LA
www.thecontentworks.com

Series design based on an original concept by Studio 183 Limited

ISBN: 978-1-84848-303-3

First edition © 2006 Thomas Cook Publishing
This third edition © 2010 Thomas Cook Publishing
Text © Thomas Cook Publishing
Maps © Thomas Cook Publishing/PCGraphics (UK) Limited
Transport map © Communicarta Limited

Series Editor: Kelly Pipes
Production/DTP: Steven Collins

Printed and bound in Spain by GraphyCems

Cover photography © TongRo Image Stock/Alamy

CONTENTS

SYMBOLS KEY

The following symbols are used throughout this book:

ⓐ address ☎ telephone ⓦ website address 🕐 opening times
🚌 public transport connections ❗ important

The following symbols are used on the maps:

ℹ️	information office	⬛	points of interest
✈️	airport	○	city
➕	hospital	○	large town
🛡️	police station	○	small town
🚌	bus station	═	motorway
🚆	railway station	▬	main road
✝️	cathedral	▬	minor road
❶	numbers denote featured	—	railway
	cafés & restaurants		

Hotels and restaurants are graded by approximate price as follows:
£ budget price **££** mid-range price **£££** expensive

▶ *Piazza Erbe's winged lion is the most famous emblem of the Veneto region*

INTRODUCING
Verona

Introduction

Shakespeare never set foot in Verona, but he gave it a widespread – although curious – claim to immortality as the home of the entirely fictional *Romeo and Juliet*. The legend continues to grow, bringing tourists from all over the world to the beautiful old walled city. Brought here in search of a myth, these tourists cannot help falling under the city's very real, enchanting spell. The old streets, elegant and intimate squares, fine Renaissance palaces, medieval castle, Roman remains and art – not to mention the warm-hearted and friendly people – give the city as romantic an appeal in real life as Shakespeare's powerful play did in fiction.

The old city centre, called the *centro storico* (historic centre), is still the heart of Veronese life, just as it was when Romans shopped in its markets, drank wine in its taverns and argued in the forum. The clothes and hairstyles may be different, but these same rhythms of life continue in modern Verona, and in much the same places.

Verona is certainly a lively city, filled with students and with young tourists that do a lot to keep its nightlife hip. OK, it's no Milan, but then it doesn't have Milan's prices or its exclusive fashionista mindset. In the summer, a lot of the action tends to move to Lake Garda, to the small towns along the eastern shore – Bardolino, Garda and Lazise. These towns are filled with people of all age groups, and the younger ones keep clubs, pubs and lakeside bars buzzing (open until late).

Few places in Italy have managed to keep the most appealing of their historic relics without becoming a static, antiquated museum. Verona, however, is home to the best-preserved Roman Arena in Italy, which is still in use for everything from grand opera to rock concerts, as well as other outstanding Roman, medieval and Renaissance sites. These both act as a backdrop and play an active role in the city.

Gucci, grand opera and gladiators join hip-hop, Shakespeare and mobile phones in a mix so comfortably blended that it's hard to draw the line between past and present.

🔺 *Past and present mingle in this lively city*

When to go

Visit Verona between April and October, when the city arches
below beautiful, blue-sky days, balmy and pleasant, with refreshing
evenings. During July and August, the city can be stiflingly hot,
and the peak of summer is a good time to join the locals, who
flee to breezy Lake Garda (see page 122) for weekends and most of
the month of August. However, unlike most Italian cities, Verona
doesn't shut down altogether during August, because this month
is the height of the opera festival (see page 12), when the Arena
hosts 15,000 opera-goers four evenings a week. Winter tends to
be chilly, but makes a fine excuse for cosying up in one of the local
restaurants, where you can take advantage of the cold weather with
a thoroughly warming menu!

SEASONS & CLIMATE

Of the many things Verona has to brag about, the weather isn't
one of them. Winter days (January and February) tend to be damp,
and average temperatures range between -2°C (28°F) and 6°C (43°F).
Thick fog often settles over the city from sunset until late morning.
Summertime (July and August) is hot and humid, with the thermometer
often hovering around 29°C (85°F). Spring and autumn are the best
seasons to visit the city, as the weather is moderate (17°C, or 63°F),
although May and October are normally also the rainiest months.

ANNUAL EVENTS
February
Carnevale di Verona (Verona Carnival) Verona's Carnival includes
parades, competitions and plenty of crazy costumes. ⓐ Piazza San
Zeno & Piazza Brà ⓣ (045) 800 0313

Verona in Love A five-day festival celebrating love and romance, including numerous performances of *Romeo and Juliet*.
📍 Various locations throughout the city 🕐 (045) 800 9461
🌐 www.veronainlove.com

March & April
Vinitaly Wine and Food Show (late Mar–early Apr) One of the biggest wine (and food) shows in Italy. 📍 Ente Autonomo Fiere di Verona, Viale del Lavoro 8 🕐 (045) 829 8111 🌐 www.vinitaly.com
ℹ Accommodation is in high demand while the show's on
Mondadori Junior Festival Cultural activities for children take place all over town. 🕐 (045) 934 952 🌐 www.mondadorijuniorfestival.it

May
Le Piazze dei Sapori Sample the flavours of Italy at this great food-fest.
📍 Piazza Brà 🕐 (045) 862 4011 🌐 www.lepiazzedeisapori.com
Festa Medioevale del Vino Bianco Soave (Soave Medieval Wine Festival) Medieval costumes are everywhere, and the wine and goodies illustrate local traditions through the ages. 📍 Soave, various locations 🕐 (045) 768 0648 🌐 www.comunesoave.it

June
Festival lirico areniano (Arena di Verona Opera) (Tues–Sun, June–Sept) Operas are staged in the 2,000-year-old Arena and draw crowds by the thousands (see page 12). 📍 Arena, Piazza Brà
🌐 www.arena.it
Festival Shakespeariano (Shakespeare Festival) (June–Aug)
A summer-long festival during which the bard's works are performed (in English) in the Teatro Romano (see page 69). 📍 Various locations
🕐 (045) 806 6485 or 806 6488 🌐 www.estateteatraleveronese.it

July
Verona Vinorum A grand exposition of the finest Veronese wines, from Soave to the Valpolicellas. ⓐ Palazzo Gran Guardia on Piazza Brà ⓣ (045) 884 0107

August
Festa del Miele (Honey Festival) Includes demonstrations and sales of honey products, plus music and entertainment. ⓐ Piazza Chiesa 1, Bosco Chiesanuova ⓣ (045) 705 0088 ⓦ www.tourism.verona.it

September
Compleanno di Giulietta (Juliet's Birthday) (16 Sept) An entirely fictitious excuse for Renaissance revelry and romantic cavorting throughout Verona. ⓐ Piazza dei Signori and Cortile Mercato Vecchio ⓣ (045) 533 115 ⓦ www.julietclub.com
Fiera dell'Uva (Grape Festival) Held in Soave at the beginning of the harvest in mid-to-late September. ⓦ www.comunesoave.it
Cura dell'Uva (Grape Cure Festival) Celebration of the wine produced in the Bardolino region from mid-September to mid-October. ⓐ Piazza del Porto, Bardolino ⓣ (045) 621 3246
Tocatì (Antique Toy Festival) Visit this three-day festival to check out an international mix of traditional toys. ⓐ Streets around Piazza Erbe ⓦ www.tocati.it

October
Maratona di Verona (Verona Marathon) Beginning in Piazza Brà, Verona's marathon sweeps through the streets. ⓣ (045) 501 531 ⓦ www.veronamarathon.it

December

Festa di Santa Lucia (mid-Dec) Stalls of goodies, called *banchéti de Santa Lùssia*, line Piazza Brà as everyone awaits the arrival of Santa Lucia with her crown of candles. ❷ Piazza Brà

Natale in Arena (Christmas Cribs in the Arena) (09.00–20.00 Dec & Jan) For almost two months, the city of Verona collects and displays nativity scenes from all over the world in the Arena. ❷ Arena di Verona ❶ (045) 592 544 ❿ www.presepiarenaverona.it

PUBLIC HOLIDAYS
Capodanno (New Year's Day) 1 Jan
La Befana (Epiphany) 6 Jan
Pasqua & Lunedi di Pasqua (Easter Sunday & Monday)
24 & 25 Apr 2011, 8 & 9 Apr 2012, 31 Mar & 1 Apr 2013
Festa della Liberazione (Liberation Day) 25 Apr
Festa del Lavoro (Labour Day) 1 May
Festa della Repubblica (Anniversary of the Republic) 2 June
Ferragosto (Feast of the Assumption) 15 Aug
Tutti Santi (All Saints' Day) 1 Nov
Festa dell'Immacolata (Feast of the Immaculate Conception)
8 Dec
Natale (Christmas) 25 Dec

On public holidays most shops and businesses will be closed and transport may run to reduced schedules. Restaurants and cafés in tourist areas may open but it is wise to check and make bookings in advance.

Opera at the Arena

In August 1913, an audience gathered in Verona's first-century Roman Arena (see page 78) to listen to a memorial performance of *Aida*. The spectacle was such a success that audiences have returned summer after summer to hear some of the world's finest artists and musicians perform opera and ballet.

The sheer size of the Arena is impressive. The stage floor alone is the largest in Europe, measuring approximately 44 m (145 ft) by 26 m (86 ft); the Arena can hold an audience of up to 20,000 people. Seating around the inside is on 45 rows (made of marble, so bring something soft to sit on). Performances don't begin until the sky is

◗ *Setting for a spectacular: the massive Roman Arena*

dark, and the surrounding area becomes a backdrop to the stage. The grand scale of the Arena allows the use of unusual stage props as well – during one performance of *Aida*, a flowing River Nile was built so that Aida could be rowed to her meeting with Radames.

Opera is the national music of Italy, and audiences span all ages. In Verona, it's regarded as popular entertainment and is not something reserved exclusively for highbrow audiences.

Opera season brings crowds to Verona from June to August. Hotel rooms are at a premium, so early booking is essential. Plan to park your car and walk into town and be sure to make reservations for pre- and post-opera dining.

Programme and tickets ⓐ Fondazione Arena di Verona, Piazza Brà 28 ⓣ (045) 800 5151 ⓦ www.arena.it

History

Location played a large part in shaping Verona's history. Situated at the outlet of the Brenner Pass, the major gateway from northern Europe, it stands at the base of the Dolomite Mountains and on the northern edge of the fertile Po valley; it was certain to be a place where cultures met and sometimes clashed.

In about 200 BC, early hunter-gatherers living in the caves of Valpolicella were overcome by the Cenomani, a Gallic-Celtic tribe allied to the Romans. As Rome gathered strength and pushed its empire northwards, it moved across the lands of the Etruscans and on into the foothills of the Dolomiti, establishing a colony at Verona in 89 BC. The strategic position of the city was ideal, and it quickly grew to be both wealthy and important. By the first century AD it was a major Roman city, with Corso Cavour created as the main Roman road into the city.

As the Roman Empire crumbled and northern tribes invaded, Verona was right in their path. The Ostrogoths arrived in 489 under King Theodoric, who promptly set up shop in a castle overlooking the city. Invading Lombards followed, before Charlemagne charged through in 774. He left his son Pepin in charge; legend has him buried under the tower of San Zeno.

In 1260 control of the city fell to Mastino I della Scala, a happy turn for the Veronese, who prospered under the rule of his family for several generations. Much of the monuments that visitors can see today were built by this powerful medieval family. The Visconti, from Milan, displaced them briefly before the Venetian Empire took charge in 1405.

Venice remained in control until it surrendered its empire to Napoleon in 1796. As Napoleon's fortunes turned, Verona was ceded to Austria; in spite of the Italian independence movement, Austria retained tight control over the entire region through the Risorgimento, until the Battle of Solferino in 1859. In 1866, Verona became a part of the new united Italy.

As an ally of England and the United States in World War I, Verona and the nearby mountain region suffered heavy attacks from Austrian armies. In World War II, after Italy abandoned its alliance with the Nazis, the former Italian dictator, Benito Mussolini, escaped to Salò on Lake Garda. Here the Germans assisted him in establishing the puppet 'Salò Republic'.

Thousands of Veronese and other northern Italians joined Resistance movements against the Germans, many paying with their lives. As the German forces withdrew in 1945, all the bridges in Verona – even the historic ones of no strategic value – were blown up.

Although heavily damaged during World War II, Verona pulled together and rebuilt many of its famed monuments. Important artists and architects have assisted in the city's renovations, including Carlo Scarpa, who revolutionised the Castelvecchio Museum (see page 86).

Verona's heritage is so rich that it could be tempted to cling to the past. As the second decade of the 21st century begins, however, new challenges force it to face the present: not least issues of climate change, the aftermath of the global economic crisis and tensions arising from immigration. No doubt the city will cope, as it has done in the past.

⬥ *Verona's Old Town sits on the Adige River*

Lifestyle

Although never considered one of Italy's most avant-garde cities, such as Turin or Milan, Verona is far from stodgy. It's a comfortable city for both residents and visitors, and perhaps most immediately striking is the mix of ages nearly everywhere. The ladies-who-lunch, Versace-clad Italo-yuppies, drowsy elderly men and college students in their designer jeans are likely to frequent the same corner bar... and smile and nod at each other as they arrive.

Although it might not have been the most egalitarian place in the past, Verona in the 21st century is a pretty democratic city, with room for all tastes, all types and all opinions (though the latter may be loudly argued through at any given opportunity). It's always been a hard-working and largely working-class city, despite the Venetian palaces and the elegant art nouveau villas across the river. What all this means for the average tourist is that he or she will be accepted, tolerated, welcomed, helped or left alone in pretty much the same proportions as they might be at home.

Verona, like the rest of Italy, is primarily Roman Catholic, although for many Veronese, this means simply attending mass at Christmas and Easter, or choosing to wed in the Catholic church. Almost entirely ethnically Italian, Verona does have a growing percentage of immigrants and expats, totalling around 8 per cent of the population. The city is not a particularly expensive place to live, paling in comparison to the high prices found in Milan, Venice or Florence. Both public transportation and the occasional meal out are very reasonable – in turn, monthly salaries are often lower than in other major Italian cities.

Despite its uncertain weather (or maybe because of it), Verona is an outdoor city, and on a nice evening or weekend afternoon it seems as though 75 per cent of the population is strolling the streets of the

Old Town. The cafés and park benches are filled to capacity, people stand around chatting, and even the steps of the two grand palaces facing the square in Piazza Brà are turned into impromptu seating.

▲ *Linger over a meal at one of the city's cosy restaurants*

Culture

Although locals are not pretentious about it, culture does play a large part in Veronese life. Wealthy patrons have always supported the city's artists, as a look inside the many churches will demonstrate. The big 'outsider' names are represented – you'll see Titian in the Duomo (see page 63) and Tintoretto in the **Chiesa di San Giorgio in Braida** (❷ Lungadige San Giorgio) – but many of these commissions came from locals, who were then able to make major names for themselves as a result of this hometown support. Regional artists such as Paolo Veronese, one of the leading Renaissance painters, and Martino da Verona, one of the great fresco artists of the 14th century, thrived in this environment. It's no wonder that the city is a UNESCO Word Heritage Site!

The Veronese are passionate about all forms of the arts, but hold opera in particularly high regard. The annual opera festival in the Arena (see page 12) is not just valued as an economic bonus, but as an important cultural resource.

Verona's civic-owned art collections are outstanding and they underscore the long history of support for the fine arts. Along with the masterpieces by Bellini and Rubens in the art museum at Castelvecchio (see page 86), there are galleries of modern art at the Palazzo Forti (see page 69) that continually feature a rotating selection of contemporary artists. Private collectors have been generous, giving back to the city where their families made their money; the most outstanding example is the Museo Miniscalchi-Erizzo (see page 68), an elegant *palazzo* full of art, priceless antique furnishings and collections of everything from armour to ivories. But culture is more than a lot of old paintings in churches and museums: it's an integral and very lively part of the local lifestyle. You'll hear music of every type – opera is not the only kind heard in the Arena, which is also a venue for major popular performers on tour.

Shakespeare's work is alive and well, and performed at the Festival Shakespeariano (see page 9). Ballet is also performed at the Teatro Romano (see page 69), along with international dance such as tango

⬤ *The cavernous passages of the Arena*

VERONA CARD

If you're in town for a few days, or interested in visiting many of the city's cultural highlights on the same day, it's wise to invest in a Verona Card. This pass costs €10 for one day or €15 for three days and entitles you to free or discounted entry to many attractions as well as free bus travel in the city. The Verona Card can be purchased at museums, churches, tobacconists and many other participating outlets. Ⓦ www.veronacard.it ❶ Note that free access to all museums is not included in the Verona Card, and some may simply offer discounts. The tourist office (see page 150) can provide an up-to-date, comprehensive list.

and flamenco. To join in the dancing yourself, head for the hills to one of Europe's best-loved indoor-outdoor discos, the Alter Ego Club (see page 76), or go to Lake Garda (see page 122), where the towns on the Verona side are known for their solid nightspots.

At any time the music options may span from concerts by Alpine choirs to traditional Mississippi folk-blues. The tourism board's website has a surprisingly complete listing, in English, at Ⓦ www.tourism.verona.it.

The tourist office in **Peschiera** (❶ (045) 755 1673) has a week-by-week listing of what's going on around Lake Garda. Find out what's happening there and in nearby, culturally buzzing Vicenza as well by picking up a free copy of *CityLights*. Listings are in Italian, but quite easy to decipher.

❶ *Centuries-old frescoes decorate façades throughout the city*

MAKING THE MOST OF
Verona

Shopping

Smart Via Mazzini, the pedestrianised street that connects Piazza Brà and Piazza Erbe, is definitely the place to shop, with big-name labels such as **Emporio Armani** (❷ Via Cappello 14) lining the route. **Prada** (❸ Porta Borsari 38) chooses the more relaxed environment of Porta Borsari, which is no slouch itself, but has a more democratic mix of shops. You'll also find hip streetwear along Via Roma, between Piazza Brà and Castelvecchio.

Shoes and leatherwear tend to be the best buys, but don't expect bargains. Do expect quality – Italian gloves are among the world's finest (but be sure they are not inferior imported ones). For quality gold and silver jewellery, go to the nearby town of Vicenza (see page 115), the capital of Italian silver- and goldsmithing. If you enjoy a good glass of wine and want to sample some of Italy's best bottles, head for the Valpolicella wine region (for red) or Soave (for white).

MARKETS

If you're partial to a cheesy souvenir or present, you won't go wrong in the market at Piazza Erbe, where you'll find such must-haves as the Juliet snowstorm paperweight and framed Capulet family tree. But sweep past the novelties and you'll come across stalls where local farmers sell cheeses and food specialities, alongside the occasional craftsman's stall where you'll find some genuine treats that will banish any thoughts of postmodern kitsch shopping.

USEFUL SHOPPING PHRASES

What time do the shops open/close?
A che ora aprono/chiudono i negozi?
Ah keh ohrah ahprohnoh/kewdohnoh ee nehgotsee?

Can I try this on?
Posso provarlo?
Pohsoh prohvarloh?

My size is ...
La mia taglia è ...
Lah meeyah tahlyah eh ...

How much is this?
Quanto costa questo?
Kwantoh kostah kwehstoh?

I'll take this one, thank you
Prenderò questo, grazie
Prehndehroh kwehstoh, grahtsyeh

Can you show me the one in the window/this one?
Può mostrarmi quello in vetrina/questo?
Poh mohstrahrmee kwehloh een vehtreenah/kwehstoh?

This is too large/too small/too expensive
Questo è troppo grande/troppo piccolo/troppo caro
Kwehstoh eh trohpoh grahndeh/trohpoh peekohloh/trohpoh kahroh

Eating & drinking

As you travel through the countryside around Verona, you'll understand why the food there is so good. Surrounded by some of northern Italy's best farmland, the Veronese countryside grows everything from asparagus and artichokes to corn for polenta and earthy mushrooms. Daily selections of fresh seafood arrive from both the Adriatic and Mediterranean ports.

Food – and the entire dining experience – is central to Italian life. Happily, you can find the same high-quality restaurants here as in Milan or Rome, but charging much lower prices. Your best bets are small family-run *trattorias* and *osterie*, where the menu may be limited but the cooking will be outstanding.

For light meals opt for bars and cafés where you can find a sandwich or *bruschette*, or shop in morning markets, such as the daily one in Piazza Erbe, buying picnic items to enjoy by the riverside. Another simple source for picnic foods is the **PAM** supermarket (ⓐ Via dei Mutilati 3 ⓣ (045) 803 2822), just off Corso Porta Nuova, through the arch on Piazza Brà.

If breakfast is not included with your room, head for a café or bar; they offer far better value than hotels. Coffee with hot milk – cappuccino or *latte macchiato* – is drunk only at breakfast. Coffee ordered at any other time will automatically be espresso unless you specify *caffè americano* (an espresso with additional hot water

PRICE CATEGORIES

Average price of a three-course meal (without drinks).

£ up to €30   ££ €30–50   £££ over €50

added) or a *caffè macchiato* (an espresso with a splash of milk).
In Italy, a bar is not just for alcoholic drinks, it's more of a café. Prices are much cheaper if you actually stand at the bar, rather than sitting at a table. If you see two prices listed for everything, the higher one is the table price.

Names for Italian eating-places can be very confusing, and there are no clear-cut definitions. A *trattoria* usually has a more limited

▲ *Take a cooling break*

and plainer menu than a *ristorante*. An *osteria* is a wine bar that serves snacks and sometimes a few dishes. Whichever type of establishment you choose, do note that if there is no menu displayed on or near the door, you should expect high prices. A *pizzeria* usually also serves a full restaurant menu. *Cucina casalinga* indicates home-style cooking.

Menus are normally divided into courses: *antipasto* (starter), *primo* (first course, usually pasta), *secondo* (second course of fish or meat) and *dolce* (pudding). A small portion of vegetables may be served alongside your *secondo*, or check the list for *contorni* – separate, larger portions of vegetables.

Verona sits in the heart of the three wine-growing regions of Soave (see page 96), Valpolicella (see page 101) and Bardolino (see page 122), which produce both everyday table wines and several distinguished ones, such as Amarone. *Vino di tavola* served by the carafe (*vino sfuso*, literally 'loose' or from the barrel) is nearly always good, and inexpensive. You can ask to sample it first.

Veronese dine late by northern European standards and most restaurants don't open for dinner until 19.30 or 20.00. Lunch is served from 12.30 until 14.30 or 15.00. At weekends or during the summer or holiday seasons, choose a place for your evening meal early and book a table (or ask your hotelier to do it). Restaurants are often closed on Sundays and Mondays. The tourist office at Piazza Brà (see page 150) has a list showing opening and closing days for individual restaurants. Finding a restaurant during August can be a challenge, so be sure to plan your meals in advance.

In most restaurants you can pay by credit card, although smaller *osterie* and *trattorie* may accept only cash. Tipping is appreciated, but is not a fixed amount. A ten per cent tip for a good meal is considered generous, and a small tip is usually added at a bar. Some restaurants, especially those in hotels, may add a service charge, listed on the bill (*servizio*), and no further tip is expected.

Although a large proportion of Italians smoke, Italy now has strict anti-smoking laws. Essentially it is now illegal to smoke in public buildings or enclosed spaces such as restaurants and bars. But you can still light up at outside tables.

USEFUL DINING PHRASES

I would like a table for ... people
Vorrei un tavolo per ... persone
Vohray oon tahvohloh pehr... pehrsohneh

Excuse me!
Scusi!
Skoozee!

May I have the bill, please?
Mi dà il conto, per favore?
Mee dah eel cohntoh, pehr fahvohreh?

Could I have it well-cooked/medium/rare please?
Potrei averlo ben cotto/mediamente cotto/al sangue, per favore?
Pohtray ahvehrloh behn kohtoh/mehdyahmehnteh kohtoh/ ahl sahngweh, pehr fahvohreh?

I am a vegetarian. Does this contain meat?
Sono vegetariano/vegetariana (fem.). Contiene carne?
Sohnoh vehjehtehrehahnoh/vehjehtehrehahnah. Kontyehneh kahrneh?

Entertainment & nightlife

There are plenty of choices for evening entertainment in Verona
and around Lake Garda. Although a little knowledge of Italian helps,
most younger people speak basic English – some quite a lot – and if
you mingle and look open to conversation, you'll soon acquire some
good local contacts who can advise you on hotspots. Try checking

● *Enjoy the casual camaraderie of the nightlife*

out Corso Porta Borsari, from the Roman gate to Piazza Erbe or near Castelvecchio.

For a music bar in stylish surrounds, begin at M27 (see page 77) on Via Mazzini, or for a casual mix go to Caffè Monte Baldo (see page 76) just off the far end of Piazza Erbe – there's no music, but people there will know where to find some any night of the week. People tend to stand in these places, which makes mixing and meeting easier. Il Campidoglio (see page 77), a bit more chic, is on Piazzetta Tirabosco, off Corso Porta Borsari.

For late music and food, head down the alley beside Sant'Anastasia to the piano bar at Madonna Verona (see page 77). Students congregate in bars and clubs near the university, across the river in Veronetta, especially at the aptly named Campus (see page 92), where a pub-like atmosphere prevails and amusements include billiards, darts and board games. Verona's well-known Alter Ego Club (see page 76), which regularly attracts European DJs, is out of town in the hills overlooking the city. For night-time entertainment with a cultural slant, surrender to a cultural infusion at Teatro Romano (see page 69) or get tickets from around €40 to hear top opera stars – under the stars. In Vicenza, Teatro Olimpico (see page 112) runs a constant programme of musical productions from April through to the autumn.

Something is always happening in the lake towns. In Bardolino, every Friday in July and August, concerts are held in the former **Chiesa della Disciplina** (🚊 Borgo Garibaldi; information from the Bardolino tourist office ❸ Piazzale Aldo Moro ☎ (045) 721 0078). Stop in at a tourist office to get lake town schedules; the one in Peschiera will have information on the east shore towns, the one in **Desenzano** (🚊 Via Porto Vecchio 34 ☎ (030) 914 1510) covers the west shore.

Sport & relaxation

With Lake Garda and the mountains so close, outdoor sports enthusiasts head north to hike, climb, sail and windsurf. Monte Baldo, east of Lake Garda, offers trails for walkers, hikers and mountain bikers.

SPECTATOR SPORTS
Football
Verona is home to two football teams – **Chievo Verona** (Ⓦ www.chievoverona.it) and **Hellas Verona** (Ⓦ www.hellasverona.it). Both play at the **Stadio Marc'Antonio Bentegodi** (ⓐ Piazzale Olimpia ⓘ (045) 577 722). Buy tickets from the official retailers listed on the Hellas site, or directly on the Chievo site.

PARTICIPATION SPORTS
Cycling
Cycling and walking paths follow the lakeshore in several places; one good one is between Bardolino and Torri del Bénaco; again, check with local tourist offices for advice and maps. In both Verona and Vicenza you can hire bicycles at the left-luggage office (*deposito bagagli*) in the railway station. Additionally, bicycles are available from **Cicli Degani**, in Lazise (ⓐ Piazzetta Beccherie 13 ⓘ (045) 647 0173 Ⓦ www.ciclidegani.com).

Golf
Arzaga Golf Club has an 18-hole par-72 course, southwest of the lake, around 65 km (40 miles) from Verona. ⓐ 25080 Carzago di Cavagese della Riviera ⓘ (030) 680 600 Ⓦ www.palazzoarzaga.com

Gardagolf Country Club has three nine-hole courses (par 35–6), and is also around 65 km (40 miles) from Verona. ⓐ Via Angelo Omodeo 2, Soiano Del Lago ⓣ (030) 680 6266 ⓦ www.gardagolf.com

Sailing & windsurfing

Boats of all sorts are available on Lake Garda, including a standard *barca* (rowing boat), *barca a vela* (sailing boat) or *motoscafo* (motorboat). Look for signs stating *noleggio* (for hire) and you're as good as afloat. To swim, look for small *piscina* (pool) or *spiaggia* (beach) signs along the shores, but don't expect to find sand. Lake beaches are more likely to be covered in small round stones.

Due to predictable winds, Lake Garda's northern waters offer excellent sailing. Hire boats in Casteletto del Brenzone, just south of Malcesine, from **Tre di Cuori Nautica** (ⓐ Via Imbarcadero 17 ⓣ (045) 743 0805 ⓦ www.nauticuore.com).

Especially in the spring and autumn, you will find windy days anywhere; a good sailing school for all ages (including a unique programme for children aged three to five) is **Fraglia Vela** (ⓐ Porto Maratona, Desenzano del Garda ⓣ (030) 914 3343 ⓦ www.fragliavela.it). For windsurfing lessons, try **VDWS Windsurfing Punta Caval** (ⓐ Torri del Bénaco, Lago di Garda ⓣ (045) 722 5215).

RELAXATION
Spas

Romans built the first spa in Sirmione, taking advantage of natural thermal springs. Today Terme di Sirmione (see page 132) has several spa centres in Sirmione, offering different services and treatments using the sulphurous spring waters. Less well known is the thermal lake in the grounds of Villa Cedri (see page 130), near Lazise, with thermal fountains, a grotto and hydromassage pools.

Accommodation

Italy's star system for accommodation helps you know what to expect, and is based on regular inspections. At 2-star hotels, for example, most or all of the rooms will have private bathrooms; 3-star establishments will have in-room telephones and television. Internet points, oddly, may be available in the most modest hotel and unavailable in a costlier one. There is usually a charge, but not always, and Wi-Fi is becoming more common in larger hotels in Verona; the San Luca (see page 35), for example, offers it throughout the building, as well as a station for guest use in the lobby.

Take location into consideration when choosing your hotel: many areas are pedestrianised and there are not always bus stops nearby. Corso Porta Nuova, between the railway station and Piazza Brà, has hotels in all price ranges and several bus stops.

Establish the rate when booking (always ask for special packages, especially at weekends), and request fax or email as proof of reservation. Be sure to have confirmed bookings for August, when locals head for the lakes and visitors fill the city for the opera festival (see page 12), and during Easter week. Some lake hotels may be closed between November and March.

PRICE CATEGORIES

Hotels in Italy are graded according to a star system (1 star for a cheap *pensione* to 5 stars for a luxurious resort with numerous facilities). Prices are for a double room, for one night, excluding breakfast unless otherwise specified.

£ up to €100   ££ €100–175   £££ over €175

⬥ *Renaissance splendour at the Due Torri Hotel Baglioni*

HOTELS

Albergo Trento £ A small and well-positioned hotel that's probably among the best bargains in town. The rooms are snug but comfortable and have private bathrooms. ➊ Corso Porta Nuova 36 (The Arena & West Verona) ➊ (045) 596 444 ➍ www.albergotrento.it ➍ Bus: 11, 12, 13

Hotel Aurora £–££ With an unbeatable location in Piazza Erbe, the Aurora offers comfortable rooms with satellite TV, private phones and air-conditioning. Most rooms and the terrace bar overlook the busy piazza. ➊ Piazza Erbe (The Old Centre) ➊ (045) 594 717 ➍ www.hotelaurora.biz ➍ Bus: 70, 71, 73

Hotel Torcolo £–££ Just steps from the Arena, yet quietly away from the city centre bustle, the Hotel Torcolo is a true find. Friendly owners have taken great care with the details and the décor, and it certainly shows. If you are on a budget, ask for a room with a *letto francese* (French bed) – both the bed, and the room, are smaller and cheaper than a standard room. ➊ Vicolo Listone 3 (The Arena & West Verona) ➊ (045) 800 7512 ➍ www.hoteltorcolo.it ➍ Bus: 11, 12, 13, 72

Hotel Martini, Hotel Piccolo ££ Both of these hotels are on the same street, a bit west of the central rail station. Modern and comfortable, either hotel is ideal if you are driving and are looking for a place with off-street parking. ➊ Via Camuzzoni 2 and 3/B (The Arena & West Verona) ➊ (045) 569 400 ➍ www.hotelsverona.it ➍ Bus: 72, 73

Hotel San Luca ££–£££ The San Luca is a simple yet refined hotel with a fabulous location just a few steps from the city's centre,

◀ *Cosy comfort in Hotel San Luca*

Piazza Brà. The hotel has covered car-park facilities with lift access to the hotel. It also has an intimate bar plus a guest lounge with a high-speed internet station. ❸ Vicolo Volto San Luca 8 (The Old Centre) ❶ (045) 591 333 ⓦ www.sanlucahotel.com ⓝ Bus: 11, 12, 13, 72

Due Torri Hotel Baglioni £££ The Due Torri is the Queen of Verona hotels. Set in a Renaissance *palazzo*, the rooms are all uniquely furnished with original 18th- and 19th-century touches, such as authentic wooden floors or antique wallpaper. Service is impeccable and the concierges do their best to obtain anything from tickets to the opera to a reservation for a romantic dinner! Pure class. ❸ Piazza Sant'Anastasia 4 (The Old Centre) ❶ (045) 595 0444 ⓦ www.baglionihotels.com

Hotel Accademia £££ Originally a 16th-century academy responsible for the schooling of upper-class youths, this gorgeous building was transformed into a hotel in 1880. Ideally located just off Via Mazzini, the city's main shopping street, guest rooms and public areas are traditionally furnished, and have internet connections and Wi-Fi. ❸ Via Scala 12 (The Old Centre) ❶ (045) 596 222 ⓦ www.accademiavr.it

BED & BREAKFASTS

Al Quadrifoglio £ A small B&B with three rooms (one with private bathroom, two sharing) in the Borgo Trento area. Rates include breakfast – and friendly hosts who generously help you to plan your daily excursions. ❸ Via XXIV Maggio 6 (The Arena & West Verona) ❶ (045) 830 0181 or 338 225 3681 ⓦ www.alquadrifoglio.it ⓝ Bus: 21, 22, 23, 24, 31, 32, 33, 41, 61, 62

Casa Coloniale £–££ With just three bright, funky rooms, Casa Coloniale plays on friendly hospitality and a fantastic central location. Highly sought after, so be sure to book early. ❸ Via Cairoli 6 (The Old Centre) ❶ (045) 801 3334 or 337 472 737 ❿ www.casa-coloniale.com ❻ Bus: 11, 12, 13, 51

HOSTELS

Ostello Santa Chiara £ Located near to the Teatro Romano and the Giusti Gardens, the Ostello Santa Chiara offers both dorm-style rooms and private doubles with en suite bathrooms. ❸ Via Santa Chiara 10 (other side of river from Old Centre) ❶ (045) 597 807 ❶ Apr–Oct ❻ Bus: 73

Ostello Villa Francescatti £ On the east side of the Adige but within walking distance of the city centre, this hostel is within a renovated 16th-century *palazzo*. Bear in mind that the hostel is fairly strict, and is closed between 09.00 and 17.00 with a curfew at 23.30. ❸ Salita Fontana del Ferro 15, off Via Fontana del Ferro (other side of river from Old Centre) ❶ (045) 590 360 ❻ Bus: 31, 32, 33

CAMPING

Camping Romeo e Giulietta £ A simple campsite, with tents and service hook-ups available. ❸ Via Bresciana 54 (outside the city) ❶ (045) 851 0243 ❿ www.turismo.veneto.it/camping ❶ Apr–Nov ❻ Bus: 13

Castel San Pietro £ An attractive area with trees overlooking the great bend of the Adige. Primarily for tents, which can be rented on site as well. ❸ Via Castel San Pietro 2 (outside the city) ❶ (045) 592 037 ❿ www.campingcastelsanpietro.com ❶ May–Sept ❻ Bus: 41, 95

THE BEST OF VERONA

Whether you are on a flying visit to Verona, or taking a more leisurely break in northern Italy, the city offers some sights and experiences that should not be missed.

TOP 10 ATTRACTIONS

- **Arena** From gladiators to grand opera, this magnificent, first-century Roman structure, located in the heart of the city, has definitely seen it all (see page 78)

- **Museo di Castelvecchio** Visit modern architect Carlo Scarpa's brilliantly designed art gallery, located in an incredible 14th-century, grand castle setting (see page 86)

- **Giardino Giusti** Wander through this Renaissance oasis, with its topiary labyrinth, positioned on the east side of the Adige River (see page 63)

- **Basilica di San Zeno** Verona's smiling saint gazes at superbly restored frescoes, ancient graffiti and magnificent bronze panels, in one of the best surviving examples of Italian Romanesque architecture (see page 80)

🔽 *The Verona Arena amphitheatre*

- **Chiesa di Santa Maria in Organo** Heavenly choir stalls, with their ornate wooden carvings, and fabulous frescoes make this often-missed 15th-century church a visual feast (see page 60)

- **Piazza dei Signori** Marvel at one of the city's most exquisite squares, complete with Dante's statue standing guard in its centre (see page 64)

- **Castel San Pietro** Hike your way up to the terrace and watch the sun go down over Verona's skyline and the Adige River (see page 59)

- **Chiesa di Sant'Anastasia** Check out the Gothic splendour of this magnificent church, commissioned by the Scaligeri family and built over a period of 200 years (see page 59)

- **Arche Scaligere** Flamboyant to the last, visit these ornate, 14th-century stone tombs, honouring Verona's leading medieval family (see page 56)

- **Teatro Romano** A Roman theatre, later jammed with townhouses, restored to its former glory and continuing to host dramas, even after 2,000 years (see page 69)

Suggested itineraries

HALF-DAY: VERONA IN A HURRY

Verona is a compact city, with many interesting sights right in the Old Town. Begin at Piazza Brà, taking time to see inside the Arena (see page 78) before following Via Roma to Castelvecchio and the Ponte Scaligero. Follow Corso Cavour past fine *palazzi* to the Roman gate of Porta Borsari. A right turn will bring you to Via Mazzini, within sight of your starting point in Piazza Brà. Or, if you have a little time when you reach Porta Borsari, continue through the gate to Piazza Erbe, the centre of Roman Verona. At the other end of the piazza, a right turn onto Via Mazzini takes you along the city's most fashionable street back to Piazza Brà.

1 DAY: TIME TO SEE A LITTLE MORE

Follow the route above to Piazza Erbe, but instead of returning on Via Mazzini, go through the arch into Piazza dei Signori. Take the lift to the top of Torre dei Lamberti (see page 66) for a view over the city, or go straight on through the piazza to see the Scaligeri Tombs (see page 56). A left turn takes you to Corso Sant'Anastasia, which leads to the church of the same name, well worth a slow peruse. Continue down the narrow passageway beside the church to the arcaded Via Sottoriva. To the right, under the arches, is the **Osteria Sottoriva** (🅐 Via Sottoriva 9/A ☎ (045) 801 4323). A right turn here takes you back to Piazza Erbe.

2–3 DAYS: TIME TO SEE MUCH MORE

If you have longer and can really explore, venture over the Ponte Pietra to Teatro Romano (see page 69) and visit the incredible inlaid choir stalls at Chiesa di Santa Maria in Organo (see page 60) before continuing on to the Giardino Giusti (see page 63). Or head in the other direction from Castelvecchio, along the river to the Basilica di San Zeno (see page 80). With the added time, be sure to spend some of it in a café in Piazza Brà – or in Piazza Erbe – and enjoy watching the local life pass by.

LONGER: ENJOYING VERONA TO THE FULL

With more time at your disposal, take in the highlights of Verona, then head for Lake Garda (see page 122). Take a drive around the southern half, using the car ferry to cross from Torri de Bénaco to Maderno, or go for a boat trip around the lake, stopping overnight in Gardone Riviera, Salò or Malcesine. If it's a weekend, you might choose to stay in Desenzano to sample some of the nightlife, or spend the time in Vicenza visiting magnificent Palladian buildings and catching a little of the evening action there.

● Ponte Scaligero, built as an escape route from Castelvecchio

Something for nothing

The free-as-sunshine nature of many of Verona's attractions means that there'll never be a need to hurl yourself onto the rocks of bankruptcy as a result of your visit.

If you are lucky enough to be in Verona on the first Sunday of the month, you can visit the following museums for free: Museo di Castelvecchio (see page 86), Museo Lapidario Maffeiano (see page 87), Tomba di Giulietta (see page 85), Museo degli Affreschi (see page 85), Teatro Romano (see page 69) and Museo Archeologico (see page 68).

Entrance to Casa di Giulietta itself (see page 56) may not be free, but entrance to its courtyard is, and you could spend many a Mills & Boon moment sighing over the hundreds of (and ever-changing) romantic notelets that are pinned to its walls – thus fostering an amorous vibe that could pay off handsomely later in the day.

Unsurprisingly, the city's parks cost nothing to enjoy, and an hour or two spent in the Giardino Giusti (see page 63) amounts to far more than a miserly cop out. The statues here are works of art in their own right and offer valuable inspiration for holiday snaps.

You don't have to be Indiana Jones to be knocked out by what's been unearthed at the Scavi Archeologici (see page 66). The finds here are fascinating, not least the massive Roman gate that reminds you why Roman wonders still cause jaws to drop today. And if that makes you want to reconsider the quiet achievements of the past, a look around nearby Chiesa di Santa Maria in Organo (see page 60) won't cost a euro. Here you'll find the work of Fra Giovanni de Verona, whose faith and devotion may not be fashionable today, but certainly bore fruit in his quite miraculously detailed marquetry. Another, much more recent, labour of love – and a symbol of the city's determination not to be cowed – in this part of the Old Town is the reconstructed

Ponte Pietra (see page 64). Local people gave their time for free to rebuild this bridge, and you can wonder at their dedication, also for free.

⬥ *Corso Porta Borsari*

When it rains

While little seems quite as grey and glowering as a rainy day in Verona, the good news is that, with the exception of the winter months, any rain is likely to leave as suddenly as it appeared.

A rainy day can be a blessing in disguise as it frees you up to abandon that sometimes over-ambitious schedule so you can actually invest some proper time in absorbing Verona's delights. You could spend hours engrossed in the religious art found in the Basilica di San Zeno (see page 80). A wet-weather pitstop in Museo di Castelvecchio (see page 86) could easily evolve into a half-day introduction to the history of Western art. If you're near the Tomba di Giulietta when the heavens open, just dive into the Museo degli Affreschi (see page 85) for a masterclass in the art of the fresco that will occupy you for hours. If you do find yourself turning into a fresco-phile, the Santa Maria Antica church (see page 60) also has some absorbing examples of the form.

The silver lining on every rain cloud is that it's an excuse to hit the shops. Unlike many Italian cities, Verona's shopping streets are not protected by porticoes, but faint heart never won great bargain, and unless there's a deluge of biblical immensity, you'll live; don't be a drip. In any case, the shops on Via Mazzini are nestled close together, so unless it rains hard, it's easy to dart between them. Or tick both 'shopping' and 'culture' off your 'to do' list in the Enoteca dell'Instituto Enologico Italiano (see page 70), where you'll enhance your appreciation of wine. Why not get ahead with your present-buying? Art and Glass (see page 70) is full of original gift ideas, and if you treat yourself to some of its eye-catching glass jewellery, you'll come out blinging in the rain.

🔺 Cangrande's statue now stands guard at Castelvecchio

On arrival

TIME DIFFERENCE
Verona, like the rest of Italy, follows Central European Time (CET).
During Daylight Savings Time (late Mar–late Oct), clocks are set
ahead one hour. Italy returns to standard CET at the end of October.

ARRIVING
By air
Verona's **Valerio Catullo Airport** (❶ (045) 809 5666
ⓦ www.aeroportoverona.it) is in Villafranca, about 12 km
(7 ½ miles) southwest of the centre. A shuttle operates every

---

IF YOU GET LOST, TRY …

Excuse me, do you speak English?
Mi scusi, parla inglese?
Mee skoozee, parrla eenglehzeh?

**Excuse me, is this the right way to the Old Town/the city
centre/the tourist office/the station/the bus station?**
Mi scusi, questa è la strada giusta per la città vecchia/il centro/
l'ufficio informazioni turistiche/la stazione ferroviaria/
la stazione degli autobus?
*Mee skoozee, kwestah eh lah strahdah justah pehr la cheetah
vehkyah/eel chentroh/loofeecho eenfohrmahtsyonee
tooreesteekah/lah statsyoneh fehrohveeahreeah/
lah statsyoneh dehlyee owtohboos?*

---

20 minutes, 06.35–11.35, between the airport and the railway station at Porta Nuova. Tickets are €4.50 (see Ⓦ www.aptv.it). A taxi to the city costs about €30.

Aeroporto di Brescia (Ⓣ (030) 204 1599 Ⓦ www.aeroportobrescia.it) is located 52 km (32 miles) from Verona, and can also be reached by shuttle bus from the city's railway station at Porta Nuova. Frequent buses run from Brescia to Salò, on Lake Garda's western shore, and trains from Brescia access both Desenzano and Peschiera on the lake, as well as Verona's Porta Nuova Station.

For additional information regarding both airports, check Ⓦ www.aeroportidelgarda.it.

By rail

Verona's **Porta Nuova railway station** (Ⓦ www.trenitalia.it) is close to the city centre and connected to Piazza Brà by bus (buy a ticket first in the bus station, opposite the railway station Ⓑ Bus: 11, 12, 13, 24, 41, 61, 72, 73). To get to the centre of Verona from the station, follow the street to the right as you exit the station, through the city gate and straight ahead along Corso Porta Nuova.

By road

Buses arrive at Porta Nuova; the bus station is located just outside the doors of the Porta Nuova train station.

If you are driving to Verona, take the A4 from Milan or Venice, and exit either at Verona Sud (Verona South) or Verona Est (Verona East). You can also head to Verona on the SS11 from Brescia, the SS12 from Lake Garda or the SS62 from Parma.

If you need a car at some point in your trip, either plan to pick it up and drop it off at the airport and use public transport into the city, or use the car rentals at the train station, convenient for major

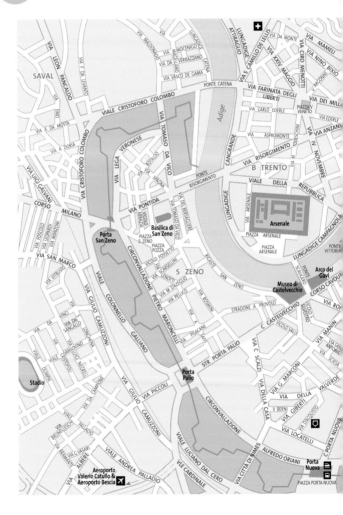

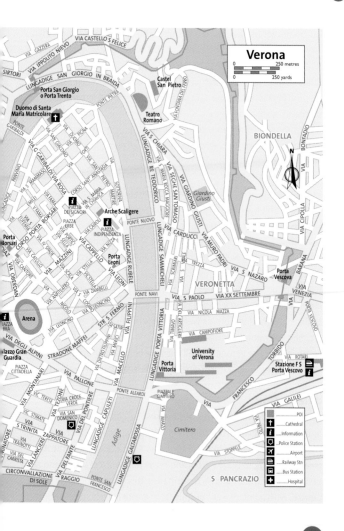

outbound routes. Routes in and out of the city are wide and well signposted. Access to the city centre is allowed only from 10.00–13.30, 16.00–18.00 and 20.00–22.00 Mon–Fri, and from 10.00–13.30 Sat & Sun. Street parking is difficult: in most areas you must buy a 'Verona Park' pre-paid card (€1.50 per hour) at a tobacconist and display it visibly on the car's dashboard.

For those visiting from the UK or Australia, remember: in Italy all traffic drives on the right.

FINDING YOUR FEET

Verona's old centre is well-kept and charming, snugly encircled by walls and the river. Life within is lively and upbeat, especially when the weather is sunny and everyone takes to the streets. Bars, cafés, restaurants, clubs, markets and shops all seem to open their doors and flow onto the well-worn paving stones of its streets, alleyways and *piazze*.

Although you should always be aware of your surroundings in any city, Verona is a relatively safe place for travellers. That said, it is wise to avoid dimly lit streets, as well as parks or deserted areas at night. Women will rarely be hassled in Verona, and certainly less than further south in Italy. The Veronese of all ages are polite and hospitable people who will answer your questions, give you directions and offer help.

ORIENTATION

Verona's Old Town is surrounded by the River Adige on three sides, and many of its key attractions are within this tightly bound area of traffic-free streets. Via Mazzini connects Piazza Brà, where the Arena (see page 78) is, to Piazza Erbe, and most of the streets between are pedestrianised. That area is described in this book under 'The Old Centre', with a line drawn roughly from Ponte Navi across to Ponte

Vittoria. Also in this section are sights on the other side of the river north of those bridges. Piazza Brà and the area around and to the south of it, as well as the long section of the city enclosed between the walls and the river west of Piazza Brà are listed in the second section, entitled 'The Arena & West Verona'. Its principal sights are connected by Via Roma, which runs between Piazza Brà and Castelvecchio, and Rigaste San Zeno, which follows the river to the outstanding church of the same name, about a 20-minute walk away. San Zeno is also connected to Castelvecchio by a bus.

The tourist office in Piazza Brà organizes walking tours of the city, a good way of getting to know Verona's layout and its cultural highlights. See ⓦ www.veronacityguide.it or call ☎ (045) 810 1322.

GETTING AROUND

Although you won't need to take a bus to most sights, local buses are available to San Zeno, Giardino Giusti and to the railway station at Porta Nuova. Route numbers may be different on Sundays, holidays and evenings, so do check ⓦ www.atv.verona.it for further information or current route changes. Buy a ticket (€1) from a news-stand or tobacconist before boarding and be sure to stamp it in the machine inside the bus when you board. A daily ticket costs €3.50. If you are travelling as a family, buy a *biglietto famiglia weekend* (€4). This return ticket, which can be used either on Saturday or Sunday, is valid for a family of four to any destination in the city. Ask at the tourist office for a copy of the bus routes and schedules, and be sure to use the *feriale* schedules on weekdays and *festivi* on Sundays and holidays.

Buses to Lake Garda are blue and depart from the bus station, right in front of the train station at Porta Nuova. Purchase tickets first inside the small bus station.

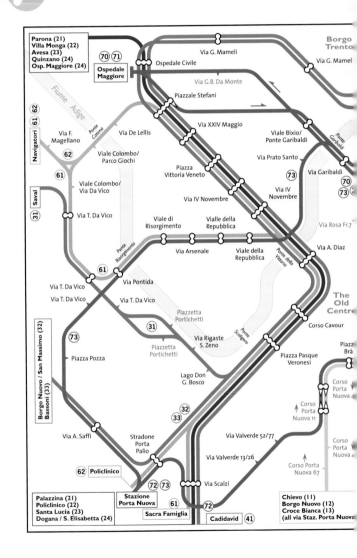

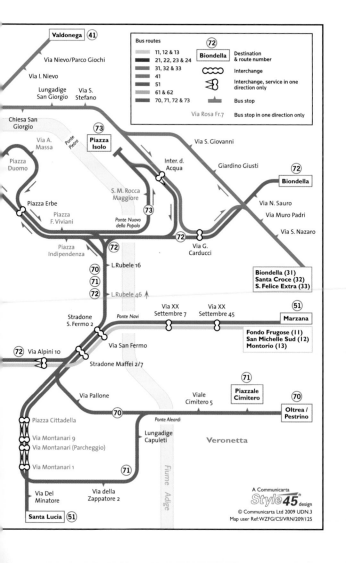

Bus routes

	11, 12 & 13	
	21, 22, 23 & 24	
	31, 32 & 33	
	41	
	51	
	61 & 62	
	70, 71, 72 & 73	

(72) **Biondella** — Destination & route number

∿∿∿ Interchange

Interchange, service in one direction only

Via Rosa Fr.7 — Bus stop

Bus stop in one direction only

Valdonega (41)

Via Nievo/Parco Giochi

Via I. Nievo

Lungadige San Giorgio

Via S. Stefano

Chiesa San Giorgio

Via A. Massa

Ponte Pietra

(73) Piazza Isolo

Via S. Giovanni

Piazza Duomo

Inter. d. Acqua

Giardino Giusti

(72) Biondella

Piazza Erbe

S. M. Rocca Maggiore

Piazza F. Viviani

Via N. Sauro

Via Muro Padri

Ponte Nuovo della Popolo

(73)

Via S. Nazaro

Piazza Indipendenza

(72)

(72)

Via G. Carducci

Biondella (31)
Santa Croce (32)
S. Felice Extra (33)

(70)

L.Rubele 16

(71)

(72)

L.Rubele 46

Via XX Settembre 7

Via XX Settembre 45

(51) Marzana

Stradone S. Fermo 2

Ponte Navi

Fondo Frugose (11)
San Michelle Sud (12)
Montorio (13)

(72) Via Alpini 10

Via San Fermo

Stradone Maffei 2/7

Via Pallone

Viale Cimitero 5

(71) Piazzale Cimitero

(70) Oltrea / Pestrino

(70)

Piazza Cittadella

Ponte Aleardi

Via Montanari 9

Lungadige Capuleti

Veronetta

Via Montanari (Parcheggio)

Via Montanari 1

(71)

Via Del Minatore

Via della Zappatore 2

Fiume Adige

Santa Lucia (51)

A Communicarta
Style 45 design
© Communicarta Ltd 2009 UDN.3
Map user Ref:WZFG/CS/VRN/209/125

The **ATV (Azienda Trasporti Verona)** now covers both transport within the city as well as buses to Lake Garda and nearby towns (☎ (045) 805 7811 🌐 www.atv.verona.it).

Taxi ranks are located at Piazza Brà, Porta Nuova rail station (see page 47), Piazza Erbe and Piazza San Zeno. Radio-dispatched taxis can be called 24 hours a day (☎ (045) 532 666). Taxis are metered, and fares within the city centre cost about €10; there is an extra charge for excess luggage.

CAR HIRE

While a car is more bother than help in the city, it is the best (and sometimes only) way to explore the surrounding areas and Lake Garda (although there are buses and even trains to the lake's principal towns). All major car hire agencies can be found at the arrivals halls of Verona Airport. Check rates before booking your flight, because you can sometimes do best with an airline's air-car package.

Before leaving the car park, be sure you have all documents. Remember to drive on the right.

Car hire offices at Verona's Valerio Catullo Airport are open 09.00–20.00, two dependable organisations being:

Avis ☎ (045) 800 6636 🌐 www.avis.it

Hertz ☎ (045) 800 0832 🌐 www.hertz.it

Car hire offices in the railway station, Porta Nuova, are normally open 08.00–12.00, 14.30–18.30 Monday to Friday and 08.00–12.00 Saturday. They are closed on Sundays.

▶ *The expanisve Piazza Brà*

THE CITY OF
Verona

The Old Centre

This is the heart of Verona, with its narrow, stone-paved streets of elegant *palazzi*, some a bit more faded than others, but all picturesque with their Venetian arched windows and frescoes. Just wandering through these pedestrianised streets is a treat. There is little bus transport in this area, but lines 70, 71 and 73 will get you to Piazza Erbe and most sights can be easily reached on foot from there. We have included public transport details where they might be useful for reaching places slightly further afield.

SIGHTS & ATTRACTIONS

Arche Scaligere (Scaligeri Tombs)

Behind Piazza dei Signori, the ornate stone tombs of Verona's leading medieval family, the della Scala, form one of the city's major Gothic art treasures. Atop the largest and grandest of these are effigies, fully armoured and on horseback. These over-the-top Scaligeri Tombs, both dating from the 1300s, almost hide the family's church, the 12th-century Santa Maria Antica (see page 60). The tombs are always visible from outside the ornate iron fence (notice the ladder worked into an ironwork pattern, the family's symbol). The interior is undergoing restoration until late 2011. ❸ Via Arche Scaligere, off Piazza dei Signori ❶ (045) 595 508 ❶ Closed for restoration until late 2011 – call for opening times

Casa di Giulietta (Juliet's House)

The restored medieval building with its 1930s balcony opens into a courtyard full of chattering tourists. Its arched passageway is covered in graffiti, and the lovely bronze statue of Juliet by sculptor

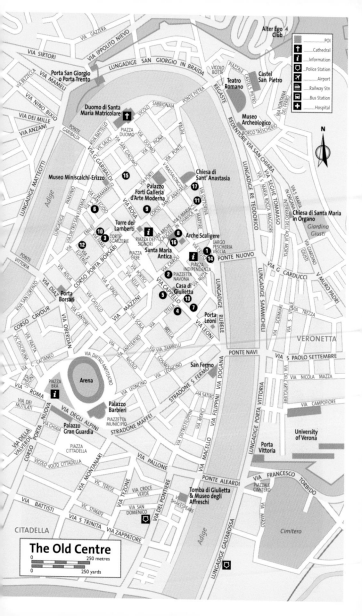

The Old Centre

```
0        250 metres
0        250 yards
```

POI
Cathedral
Information
Police Station
Airport
Railway Stn
Bus Station
Hospital

N

Alter Ego Club

VIA GAZZERA

VIA SIRTORI

VIA IPPOLITO NIEVO

LUNGADIGE SAN GIORGIO IN BRAIDA

VICOLO BOTTE

PIAZZALE CASTEL S. PIETRO

Castel San Pietro

Teatro Romano

VIA BEZZECCA

VIA MAMELI

Porta San Giorgio o Porta Trento

VICOLO CASTEL S. PIETRO

PONTE PIETRA

VICOLO SABBIONAIA

VIA PIETRA

REGASTE REDENTORE

Museo Archeologico

BORGO TASSCHERO

VIA NINO BIXIO

VIA DEI MILLE

VIA ANZANI

Duomo di Santa Maria Matricolare

PIAZZA DUOMO

VIA DUOMO

VIA PONTE PIGNA

VASSALONCELLO

VIA SOTTORIVA

VIA S. CHIARA

LUNGADIGE RE TEODORICO

VIA S. MARIA ROCCA MAGGIORE

VIA SECHE TOMMASO

VIA GARIBALDI

VIA BATTELLO

VIA VICALOLO

VIA SAN GIACOMO

Chiesa di Sant'Anastasia

Chiesa di Santa Maria in Organo

Giardino Giusti

Museo Miniscalchi-Erizzo

15

VIA G. GARIBALDI

VIA ROSA

VIA S. MAMMOLO

CORSO

Palazzo Forti Galleria d'Arte Moderna

9

17

VIA S. ANASTASIA

VIA SANTA CATERINA

LUNGADIGE MATTEOTTI

Adige

PONTE VITTORIA

6

VIA S. CANOSSIANE

VIA PANTANO

EMILEI

Torre dei Lamberti

CORTE SGARZERIE

10 3

8

Arche Scaligere

16

VIA MINI PIANA

VIA CHIAVA MARTINI

LUNGADIGE SAMMICHELI

12

CORSO PORTA BORSARI

PIAZZA DELLE ERBE

PIAZZA DEI SIGNORI

Santa Maria Antica

1

LARGO PESCHERIA VECCHIA

14

PONTE NUOVO

VIA G. CARDUCCI

VERONETTA

Porta Borsari

VIA ADUA

VIA CATULLO

VIA SPADE

VIA MAZZINI

VIA CAPPELLO

VIA STELLA

2

PIAZZETTA NAVONA

PIAZZA INDIPENDENZA

9

13

Casa di Giulietta

LUNGADIGE RUBELE

VIA MURO PADRI

VIA TREZZA

RIVA SAN LORENZO

VIA DIAZ

CORSO CAVOUR

VIA OBERDAN

VIA DISCIPLINA

VIA TRATTA

CATTANEO

4

7

Porta Leoni

VIA LEONI

PONTE NAVI

VIA S PAOLO SETTEMBRE

VIA DEL PONTIERE

VIA NICOLA MAZZA

VIA ROMA

PIAZZA BRA

Arena

VIA DIETRO ANFITEATRO

VIA LEONCINO

VIA ANFITEATRO

San Fermo

STRADONE S. FERMO

VIA DOGANA

VIA FILIPPINI

VIA SATIRO

VIA CAMPOFIORE

University of Verona

VIA DEI MUTILATI

VIA DEGLI ALPINI

Palazzo Barbieri

PIAZZETTA MUNICIPIO

STRADONE MAFFEI

VIA MACELLO

VIA DIETRO FILIPPINI

LUNGADIGE PORTA VITTORIA

Porta Vittoria

PIAZZALE CIMITERO

Palazzo Gran Guardia

VIA DELLA VALVERDE

CORSO PORTA NUOVA

VIA GHIAIA

PIAZZA CITTADELLA

VICOLO VOLTO CITTADELLA

VIA PALLONE

PONTE ALEARDI

VIA FRANCESCO TORBIDO

Cimitero

CITADELLA

VIA BATTISTI

VIA MONTANARI

VIC TERESE

VIA CROCE VERDE

VIC STIMATE

VIA SAN DOMENICO

VIA S TRINITA

VIA ZAPPATORE

VIA SHAKESPEARE

Tomba di Giulietta & Museo degli Affreschi

LUNGADIGE CAPULETTI

VIA MAZZO

Nereo Costantini is kept shiny (or at least one part of it is) by hundreds of thousands of hands. Inside, the house is an interesting look at domestic architecture, with some period furnishings and cinematic memorabilia. ⓐ Via Cappello 23 ⓣ (045) 803 4303 ⓛ 08.30–19.30 Tues–Sun, 13.30–19.30 Mon (last entry 18.45). Admission charge (courtyard free)

Castel San Pietro

At the end of the Ponte Pietra, a stepped passageway leads up – and up – to the castle, a much-rebuilt affair that was originally built by King Theodoric, on a site that had been fortified by the Romans. The castle itself isn't open, nor is it the purpose of the climb. From the terrace before it is a breath-taking view of Verona, embraced snugly by the Adige. While the sunset views from any height on this side of the river are good, this is the favourite spot for the Veronese to watch their city fade into evening shadows. ⓐ Piazzale Castel San Pietro (accessed via Vicolo Botte) ⓝ Bus: 31, 32, 33

Chiesa di Sant'Anastasia

It's hard to find things in Verona that are not connected to the Scala family, since the Scaligeri had a hand in nearly everything: this church was commissioned by them around 1290 and took close to two centuries to build. Whole sections of it were removed when Napoleonic troops pillaged the city for booty to take back to Paris, but plenty of its Gothic splendour remains, and a major restoration project has left it gleaming. Just inside the door is a pair of very unusual holy water fonts. Another highlight is the Pisanello fresco of Saint George and the Princess. ⓐ Piazza Sant'Anastasia, off Corso

ⓞ *The 14th-century Scaligeri Tombs*

Sant'Anastasia ☎ (045) 592 813 🌐 www.chieseverona.it
🕐 09.00–18.00 Mon–Sat, 13.00–18.00 Sun, Mar–Oct; 10.00–13.00,
13.30–17.00 Tues–Sat, 13.00–17.00 Sun, Nov–Feb. Admission charge

Chiesa di Santa Maria Antica

The small Romanesque church of Santa Maria Antica, consecrated
in 1185, was the family church of the della Scala family, and the
tomb of the patriarch Cangrande I is set into the outside wall, over
the church's door. The inside is plain, except for bits of 14th-century
fresco and the 13th-century frescoes inside the apse. ❸ Via Arche
Scaligere, behind Piazza dei Signori ☎ (045) 595 508 🕐 07.30–12.30,
15.30–19.00. Admission charge

Chiesa di Santa Maria in Organo

Although the interior of the 15th-century church is lavishly decorated
in fresco work, the few visitors who seek out this church across the
river head straight for the choir stalls. These are decorated with
amazingly detailed inlaid wood panels created between 1477 and
1501 by the monk, Fra Giovanni da Verona. It is hard to imagine that
marquetry work could be so fine as to make bird feathers look real
and objects appear to be three-dimensional. Scenes from old Verona
alternate with simulated display cupboards filled with everyday
objects; others show lifelike creatures. These panels continue in the
sacristy, accessed by a door from the left of the choir. Be sure to look
up at the fine frescoes that make the room appear to be galleried,
with clerics and nuns watching the activity below. ❸ Piazza Isolo
Sorge, off Via Santa Chiara ☎ (045) 591 440 🕐 09.00–12.00,
15.00–18.00 🚍 Bus: 72

▶ *Escape the bustle in the Giardino Giusti*

Duomo di Santa Maria Matricolare

Verona's cathedral is, like many Italian churches, a sampler of the styles current at the time of its various reconstructions – Romanesque, Gothic and Renaissance. The site is older than any of these, first a Roman temple, then a fifth-century church. What you see now was begun in 1139, and the double-storey Romanesque portal with its sombre stone saints dates from those medieval times. The cathedral's artistic highlight is in the first chapel on the left which contains Titian's 1530 *Assumption*. The choir screen, by Michele Sanmicheli (1484–1559), who designed many of Verona's palaces, is also worth a look. ❸ Piazza Duomo ❶ (045) 595 627 ❷ 10.00–17.30 Mon–Sat, 13.30–17.00 Sun, Mar–Oct; 10.00–16.00 Tues–Sat, 13.30–17.00 Sun, Nov–Feb ❷ Bus: 73. Admission charge

Giardino Giusti (Giusti Gardens)

Counted among the finest Renaissance gardens in Italy, the 15th-century Giusti Gardens are a green oasis on the east side of the river. Peaceful lower lawns with statues and *parterres* give way to a wilder hillside where paths climb through the trees, giving views over the neatly trimmed gardens and dark cypresses below. At the very top, a grotesque carved face forms a balcony. At one side of the lower garden is a hedge maze that few can resist pitching their wits against. ❸ Via Giardino Giusti 2 ❶ (045) 803 4029 ❷ 09.00–20.00 (summer); 09.00–sunset (winter) ❷ Bus: 31, 32, 33. Admission charge

Piazza Erbe

More intimate and medieval in feeling than the grand Piazza Brà, this older square, surrounded by colourfully frescoed buildings, has

❮ *Piazza Erbe lies at the heart of Verona's historical centre* been a marketplace for at least 2,000 years. At its centre, usually hard to see because of the market stalls that almost enclose it, the Madonna of Verona atop the fountain is a Roman statue given a halo and new holier persona in 1368. The Lion of St Mark with its book, surveying the busy market from a column at the end, is a reminder that Verona was part of the Venetian Empire during the glory days of the Renaissance. Palazzo Mafei, behind the lion, is 17th century, despite the latter-day Roman gods on its façade. On weekday mornings the square is filled with food vendors, replaced by souvenir hawkers much of the rest of the time. At night, the surrounding cafés spill even further into the square, turning it into a giant cocktail party. ⊘ Bus: 70, 71, 73

Piazza dei Signori

A truly beautiful square in the centre of the Old Town, look out for splendid Renaissance Loggia del Consiglia and other elegant buildings that frame this enclosed space next to Piazza Erbe. A large statue of Dante marks the square's centre, as Dante lived in Verona during his exile from Florence.

Ponte Pietra (Pietra, or 'Stone' Bridge)

On 25 April 1945, the retreating German army mined the ancient Ponte Pietra, along with the larger bridges over the Adige, before leaving the city. A decade later, after essential services had finally been restored, the Veronese set about reconstructing their favourite bridge from the stones they had carefully salvaged from the river. The bridge the Germans destroyed had already had a tumultuous history, with recurring floods destroying several of its arches, which

---

◗ *Ponte Pietra, painstakingly rebuilt after the war*

were rebuilt at various times. The two arches closest to Teatro Romano (see page 69) were Roman; the one closest to the city bank was built in 1298 and the middle two had been rebuilt in 1520. The painstaking reconstruction is faithful in every detail to the one that was destroyed. Ⓝ Bus: 31, 32, 33

Scavi Archeologici (Archaeological Excavations) & Roman Gates

Whenever any building project requires excavation, new pieces of Verona's Roman past emerge from beneath its streets and buildings. The foundations of a massive Roman gate have been unearthed under Via Cappello, off Piazza Erbe, and left exposed so you can see the stonework and match it with the diagram of the whole structure on the facing wall. On the other side of the wall is one complete arch of the original gate, Porta Leoni, which had been incorporated into the side of a building.

At the other end of Piazza Erbe, Via Corso Porta Borsari leads to another original first-century Roman gate, Porta Borsari. Beyond, on Corso Cavour, is the Arco dei Gavi (Gavi Arch, see page 78), one of the finest examples of its period.

Torre dei Lamberti (Lamberti Tower)

Rising above Piazza dei Signori and Piazza Erbe, the Lamberti Tower marks the location of the medieval palace used as law courts, now under major restoration. Climb the tower (if you're in good shape), or pay a euro more for the lift to look down onto the Arena, the umbrellas of Piazza Erbe and for views of the snowcapped peaks of the Dolomites. Ⓐ Via dalla Costa 1, between Piazza Erbe & Piazza dei Signori Ⓣ (045) 927 3027 Ⓛ 08.30–20.30 Mar–Oct; 08.30–19.30 Nov–Feb. Admission charge

JULIET, ROMEO'S MISSUS, VERONA'S MYTH

There's not a lick of truth to it, but the tragic tale of *Romeo and Juliet* has become the world's most enduring love story, retold in opera, ballet, film – and even a Broadway musical. But the plot did not begin with Shakespeare, or in Verona. In 1530, Luigi da Porto chose the names of two Vicenza families, the Montecchi and Capelletti, for his characters, perhaps inspired by two castles above nearby Montecchio Maggiore (see page 94). In 1562, British poet Arthur Brooke published his 3,000-line translation of the story. This drew William Shakespeare's attention, and his play, set in Verona, is considered the best version of the tale; certainly it's the best known.

Verona has a love-hate relationship with these fictional residents. While shopkeepers make euros on souvenirs and hotels (even pastry shops) promote the romantic pair, locals privately roll their eyes at the hordes of giggling teens who grasp the right breast of the bronze Juliet for photographs beneath the balcony (touching the statue is supposed to bring good fortune). Never mind that the balcony was put there in the 1930s by a government bent on creating its own myths, or that the house was chosen because it was once owned by a family whose name sounded something like Capulet. Try as Verona does to be honest (the city's website has a very accurate account), the myth has a life of its own.

So the Veronese shrug and play along, obligingly designating an unoccupied tomb as Juliet's (see page 85) and smiling indulgently as the **Juliet Club** (W www.julietclub.com) affixes plaques claiming buildings as locations of various scenes from the play.

CULTURE

Verona's treasures, for the most part, are not collected into
museums, and even when they are, the attraction is often as
much in the setting – a fine *palazzo* or a crumbling convent –
as in the collections themselves.

Museo Archeologico (Archaeological Museum)

The former monastery of St Jerome, above Teatro Romano, houses
the small Archaeological Museum filled with Roman statues, reliefs,
columns, mosaics, bronzes, pottery and glass. In the tiny San Girolamo
church, part of the museum, are frescoes dating from the 15th and
16th centuries. Views down onto Verona from the museum's outdoor
terraces are best photographed in the morning, when the sun hits
the colourful old houses along the opposite river bank. ❸ Regaste
Redentore 2 ❶ (045) 800 0360 ❶ 08.30–19.30 Tues–Sun, 13.30–19.30
Mon (last entry 18.45) ❷ Bus: 31, 32, 33. Admission charge

Museo Miniscalchi-Erizzo (Miniscalchi-Erizzo Museum)

One of the city's most overlooked museums, this delightful family
collection is housed in their late-Gothic *palazzo* – which is in itself
well worth seeing. The exhibits include several different collections,
each interesting on its own; taken together they form a remarkable
museum. The subjects cover archaeology, armour and weapons of
the Renaissance, ivories and porcelain, and are shown amid the
Venetian 18th-century furniture and paintings that filled the rooms.
Highlights include the library and Ludovico Moscardo's 'Wunderkammer',
a room of curiosities assembled by a 17th-century scholar and
traveller. Look at the outside of the *palazzo* to see the original 1590
frescoes on the façade, some of which mimic architectural features

– statues, niches, columns and windows. ❸ Via San Mammaso 2/A
❶ (045) 803 2484 Ⓦ www.museo-miniscalchi.it ❶ 11.00–13.00,
16.00–19.00 Sun–Fri, Oct–May; 11.00–13.00 Sun–Fri, June–Sept
Ⓝ Bus: 70, 71. Admission charge

Palazzo Forti Galleria d'Arte Moderna (Modern Art Museum)

Regional artists of the past two centuries are featured, along
with changing exhibitions of contemporary works and those in
the civic collections. Good for art enthusiasts, but a likely skip for
others, since there are no blockbusters here. ❸ Volto Due Mori 4,
off Corso Sant'Anastasia ❶ (045) 800 1903 Ⓦ www.palazzoforti.it
❶ 10.30–19.00 Tues–Sun Ⓝ Bus: 70, 71. Admission charge

Teatro Romano (Roman Theatre)

Two thousand years ago, Romans watched performances at
this theatre built into the natural curve of the hillside; then,
over the centuries, the area was built over with homes and
shops until no trace of the theatre remained. In 1830, a Veronese
merchant purchased the land and buildings and began the task
of uncovering the amphitheatre. It is in use once again, with a
summer Shakespeare festival (see page 9), ballet and jazz concerts.
The former monastery above houses the small Museo Archeologico
(Archaeological Museum, see page 68). ❸ Regaste Redentore 2
❶ (045) 800 0360 ❶ 08.30–19.30 Tues–Sun, 13.30–19.30 Mon
(last entry 18.45) Ⓝ Bus: 31, 32, 33. Admission charge

RETAIL THERAPY

Via Mazzini is the street. Most of the big names – **Furla** (❸ Via
Mazzini 55 ❶ (045) 800 4760 Ⓦ www.furla.com), **Louis Vuitton**

(🅐 Via Mazzini 82 ☎ (045) 801 2305 🅦 www.louisvuitton.com),
Gucci (🅐 Via Mazzini 34 ☎ (045) 803 3827 🅦 www.gucci.com) – line
either side. Prices are as high as the fashion, mitigated by twice-yearly
sales from mid-July to August and again in January. Corso Porta
Borsari has more of these stylish shops, but with some less pricey
options, especially for shoes. On the second Saturday of each month
Mercato di Sottoriva turns Via Sottoriva into an antiques market.

Bene Pick up unusual glass jewellery or funky mobiles, created by
local artist Benedetta Giusti. 🅐 Via Ponte Pietra 3/A ☎ (045) 801 3411
🅦 www.beneartglass.com 🕑 10.00–12.30, 15.30–19.30 Tues–Sat

Caffè Tubino Breeze past this tiny coffee shop and you may mistake
it for just another bar. But besides over 100 types of coffee, there's
a huge and fantastical range of unusual coffee cups and pots.
🅐 Corso Porta Borsari 15/D ☎ (045) 803 2296 🕑 06.00–00.00
Mon–Sat, occasional openings Sun

Dischi Volanti Whatever your taste in music, you'll be overwhelmed
with the choices here. Staff can help you to find out where the local
live music is, too. 🅐 Via Fama 7/A ☎ (045) 801 2531 🕑 15.30–19.30 Mon,
09.30–12.30, 15.00–19.30 Tues–Sat

Enoteca dell'Instituto Enologico Italiano The Italian Wine Institute
owns and manages two expensive shops, one in Verona and another
in Soave. Friendly staff will answer any wine-related questions
or prepare tastings. 🅐 Via Sottoriva 7/B ☎ (045) 590 366
🅦 www.enotecaverona.com 🕑 14.30–19.30 Mon, 09.30–12.30,
15.30–19.30 Tues–Sat

Erboristeria Città Antica Nestled at the back of one of Verona's side streets, this organic herbal shop creates personalised teas. Wonderful honeys and essential oils are also for sale. ❹ Vicolo cieco Racchetta 6, off Via Cappello ❶ (045) 800 2826 Ⓦ www.erboristeriacittaantica.com 🕒 09.30–12.30, 15.45–19.30 Mon–Sat

Libreria Grosso Ghelfi & Barbato A venerable bookstore with a good selection of maps and travel books, as well as some general reading in English. ❹ Via Mazzini 21 ❶ (045) 800 2306 🕒 10.00–19.30 Mon–Sat

Love Therapy A department store for the cool-at-heart, with Sunday shopping and everything from designer jeans to writing paper – and brands like Miss Sixty, Diesel and Energie. ❹ Via Mazzini 6 ❶ (045) 596 577 🕒 09.00–19.30

Mr Gulliver From flight jackets to well-worn jeans, this retro/second-hand shop in the low-rent district across the river (take Ponte Navi) offers quirky wearables and military surplus at fair prices. ❹ Via San Vitale 7/E ❶ (045) 801 5642 Ⓦ www.mrgulliver.net 🕒 10.00–12.30 Tues–Sat, 15.30–19.30 Mon–Sat

My Collection Contemporary paintings, drawings, art prints and photograpy, not just for the serious collector. ❹ Via Sottoriva 12 ❶ (045) 801 3966 🕒 10.00–13.00, 16.00–20.00 Tues–Sat

TAKING A BREAK

Finding a café with chairs to sink into is not a problem in old Verona, where you are never far from Piazza Erbe. Many more hide in the nearby small streets and squares.

Art & Chocolate £ ❶ Part chocolate shop, part bar, part art gallery with a rotating selection of temporary exhibitions – an unusual mix, but it works. The space is clean and bright, with white walls and contemporary lines. ⓐ Largo Pescheria Vecchia 9/A ❶ (045) 800 1212 ❺ 08.00–02.00 Mon, Wed–Sat, 15.00–21.00 Sun

Caffè Malta £ ❷ Sitting on the tiny Piazzetta Navona, Caffè Malta is heaving on weekend nights, when the crowd is young and lively. Go during the early evening to snag a seat by the fountain. ⓐ Piazzetta Navona 8/A ❶ (045) 803 0530 ❺ 07.30–02.00 Tues–Sun

G&G Drink & Food £ ❸ With red walls and exposed brick, this relaxed bar serves light snacks throughout the day, including specialities from Le Marche, like stuffed olives. ⓐ Via Fama 6/B ❶ (045) 800 9660 ❺ 07.30–21.30 Mon–Sat

Gastronomia Stella £ ❹ On a sunny day, pick up a picnic lunch and head for one of the city's many green open spaces. This deli makes its own *baccala alla vicentina* (Vicenese salt cod) and *carciofi alla romana* (Roman artichokes). ⓐ Via Stella 11/A ❶ (045) 806 8169 ❺ 08.00–13.00 Mon–Sat, 16.00–19.30 Mon & Tues, Thur–Sat

Locandina Cappello £ ❺ One of the hottest spots in Verona's Old Town, go for a glass of wine in the evening or their amazing open sandwiches any time of day. ⓐ Via Cappello 16 ❶ (045) 803 5218 ⓦ www.locandinacappello.it ❺ 10.00–21.00 Sun–Fri, 10.00–22.00 Sat

Osteria Le Petarine £ ❻ A little *osteria/enoteca* (wine shop) where you can join locals for a glass of wine – or an inexpensive lunch or bar snack. ⓐ Via San Mammaso 6/A ① (045) 594 453 ● 07.00–21.00 Mon–Fri, 07.00–13.30 Sat

Pasticceria Cordioli £ ❼ There's standing room only at this old-style pastry shop and coffee bar. Choose a couple of the many delectable pastries made on site, order a coffee and take your snack to one of the high tables. ⓐ Via Cappello 39 ① (045) 800 3055 ● 07.30–12.45 Thur–Tues, 15.00–19.30 Mon & Tues, Thur–Sat

AFTER DARK

A university and plenty of young tourists keep Verona lively at night. After a long *aperitivo* 'hour' after work, locals head to small intimate *osterie* and *trattorias* in the streets of the old city. These are easy to spot when the weather is nice, since most extend their dining rooms into the street.

RESTAURANTS

Don't be misled by the names – in Verona there's often little difference between a *trattoria* and a *ristorante*, and little *osterie* may offer some surprisingly sophisticated fare.

Hostaria La Vecchia Fontanina £ ❽ Somewhat difficult to find but well worth the wander, the tiny *hostaria* serves up unusual local delights, like vegetable strudel in a parmesan sauce, at bargain prices. ⓐ Piazzetta Chiavica 5, down Via San Pietro Martire from Piazza Sant'Anastasia ① (045) 591 159 ⓦ www.vecchiafontanina.it ● 12.00–14.30, 19.00–22.30

Giulietta e Romeo £–££ ❾ An *osteria* and *enoteca*, priding itself on its choice of wines, this local spot is often packed out on weekend nights. Go early to secure a spot at one of the checked tables. ⓐ Corso Sant'Anastasia 27 ⓣ (045) 800 9177 ⓛ 12.15–14.30 Tues–Sat, 18.45–22.30 Mon–Sat

Osteria Sgarzarie £–££ ❿ Set in a romantic courtyard just off Piazza Erbe, this mid-range restaurant serves excellent food and fine local wines. ⓐ Corte Sgarzarie 14/A ⓣ (045) 800 0312 ⓦ www.sgarzarie.it ⓛ 12.30–14.00, 19.00–01.00 Tues–Sun ⓝ Bus: 72, 73

Osteria Sottoriva £–££ ⓫ Tucked under the picturesque *portici* of a narrow street, this *osteria* has plenty of atmosphere, good food and a friendly crowd. ⓐ Via Sottoriva 9/A ⓣ (045) 801 4323 ⓛ 12.00–15.30, 18.30–22.30

Ristorante Sant'Eufemia £–££ ⓬ Serving up an extensive menu of traditional recipes, including *bollito misto Veronese di carne* (mixed Veronese poached meats), the best reason to visit Ristorante Sant'Eufemia is the outdoor terrace and its long corridor of tables, sitting snugly between two buildings. ⓐ Via Emilei 21/B ⓣ (045) 800 6865 ⓦ www.s.eufemia.it ⓛ 12.30–14.30, 19.30–22.30 Mon–Sat

La Taverna di Via Stella £–££ ⓭ A friendly little restaurant serving regional specialities like stuffed duck and a wide variety of polenta dishes. The staff are outstanding, the wine list is massive and the ambience is cosy. ⓐ Via Stella 5/C ⓣ (045) 800 8008 ⓛ 12.15–14.30 Tues, Thur–Sun, 19.15–23.00 Thur–Tues

Trattoria alla Colonna £–££ ⓮ Don't be surprised to see donkey (*asino*) on the menu – it's a local delicacy – served as a sauce for the pasta or as a stew. The more conservative can find rabbit, trout and very generous portions of veal. This restaurant, near the Scaligeri Tombs, also offers an extensive wine list. **ⓐ** Largo Pescheria Veccia 4 **ⓣ** (045) 596 718 **ⓛ** 19.30–23.30

Trattoria alla Pigna £–££ ⓯ Put this dining room high on your list. Classy enough for a big date, its prices are low and the food excellent. Go for the *nodini di vitello con asparagi* – tender scallops of veal with asparagus – or for the *tagliata di manzo con rucola e grana*, slices of rare beef fillet on a bed of tangy greens with cheese shavings. Book ahead at weekends, since locals fill it fast. **ⓐ** Via Pigna 4/B **ⓣ** (045) 800 4080 **ⓛ** 12.30–14.30, 19.15–22.30 Tues–Sat, 12.30–14.30 Sun

Osteria al Duca ££ ⓰ Boasting a prime location in the same building as Romeo's 'home', Osteria al Duca serves up excellent traditional Veronese fare. **ⓐ** Via Arche Scaligere 2 **ⓣ** (045) 594 474 **ⓛ** 12.15–14.30, 18.45–22.30 Mon, Wed–Sat, 18.45–22.30 Tues

Due Torri £££ ⓱ For a big night out, pull out all the stops and go for broke at this elegant dining room in a Renaissance palace. Service is as good as the menu, which changes often to highlight local vegetables, meats and seafood. The lamb chops are always excellent, as is the daily risotto. **ⓐ** Piazza Sant' Anastasia 4 **ⓣ** (045) 595 044 **ⓦ** www.baglionihotels.com **ⓛ** 12.30–14.30, 19.30–22.00 **ⓘ** Booking essential

BARS & CLUBS

Two popular meeting places in this part of the city are at either end of Corso Porta Borsari: Piazza Erbe, where cafés and bars spill out onto the street in the evening, and near the Roman gate at the opposite end of the street. Check out the area to find the night's most lively spots, making sure to peek down tiny side streets.

Alter Ego Club Even people who have never been to Verona have heard of this club. It's the city's most hip and edgy, with top European DJs, although the view from the terrace in the summer is more along the lines of gooey romantic, overlooking the city lights from the northern hills. If you haven't got a car, hop on one of the free *navettes*, or bus services, that depart from the Porta Nuova train station every 40 minutes. ➌ Via Torricelle 9 ➊ (045) 915 130 ➍ www.alteregoclub.it ➎ 23.30–04.00 Fri & Sat

Caffè delle Erbe While you would expect a café with tables reaching into Piazza Erbe to be the haunt of tourists, it's actually an after-hours favourite of the young professional set, who go for the good cocktails, good company and, in the summer, for the live jazz. It tends to be quieter during the daytime. ➌ Piazza Erbe 32 ➊ (045) 591 403 ➎ 07.30–02.00 Tues–Sun

Caffè Monte Baldo This very popular and casual wine bar attracts a friendly crowd and boasts a good list of wines in all price ranges. Although furnished with little tables in the front room and bigger booths in the back, most stand at the bar or in the street. Stop in on a Friday or Saturday for a plate of oysters. ➌ Via Rosa 12 (near Piazza Erbe) ➊ (045) 803 0579 ➎ 10.00–15.00, 17.00–21.00 Tues–Sun, June–Aug; 10.00–15.00, 17.00–21.00 Mon–Sat, Sept–May

Camelot Surprisingly, the winding rooms decked out with medieval Irish décor seem to fit right into the Verona scene. Staff are friendly and there is a large-screen TV for sporting events. 🅐 Via Leoncino 7 🛈 (045) 800 1096 🕑 17.00–02.00 Tues–Sun

Il Campidoglio Not very many tourists find this chic, friendly local bar, although it's only a few steps off Corso Porta Borsari. Try one of their popular Caribbean-themed cocktails. 🅐 Piazzetta Tirabosco 4 🛈 (045) 591 059 🕑 11.00–02.00 Tues–Sun

M27 Stylish and upmarket (this is, after all, Verona's most fashionable street), this very popular wine and music bar is also a disco. It serves the best (and maybe only) club sandwiches in town. 🅐 Via Mazzini 27 🛈 (045) 800 1339 🕑 08.30–02.00 Tues–Sun

Madonna Verona A stylish little piano bar that serves light food into the wee hours, it's the perfect romantic after-dinner stop. 🅐 Via don Bassi 4, beside the Due Torri Hotel and Sant' Anastasia 🛈 (045) 595 040 🕑 12.00–15.00, 18.00–04.00

The Arena & West Verona

Elegant, spacious Piazza Brà marks the boundary between the close-set old streets and lanes of the old city and the broader avenues of the later city to its south. Free from the constriction of the river's tight bend, this area has a more spacious feel.

SIGHTS & ATTRACTIONS

Not so closely packed as those of the old centre, attractions here are conveniently connected by bus lines, easy to use in Verona as long as you remember to buy your ticket in advance (at news-stands or tobacconists) and to validate it in the machine as soon as you board.

Arco dei Gavi (Gavi Arch)

Close to Castelvecchio on Corso Cavour is the Arco dei Gavi (Gavi Arch), a first-century Roman gateway complete with its roadway, showing the grooves made by chariot wheels passing through it. You may wonder why there was so much traffic through a gate that led right into the river. Well, this is not the gate's original site – it was moved here in the 1930s. Ⓝ Bus: 21, 22, 23, 24, 31, 32, 33, 41, 61, 62

Arena

Standing at the top tier of the immense Arena (it held over 22,000 people when it was built in the first century AD) and looking down – way down – into the ring where gladiators once fought for their lives, it's easy to imagine the glory that was Rome. Whether you side with the lions or the Christians, you cannot help but think of the enormity of the spectacle and of the events that took place here as you stand in Italy's best-preserved Roman arena. It has been part

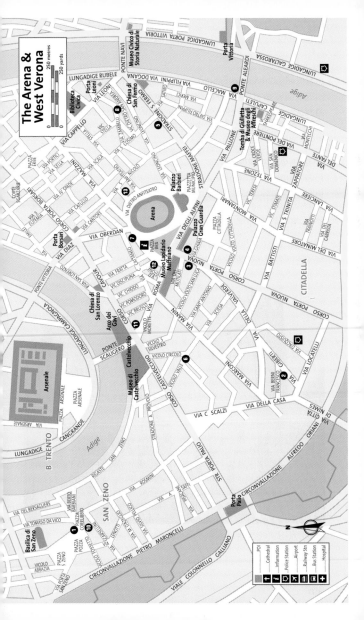

The Arena & West Verona

0 250 metres
0 250 yards

LUNGADIGE RUBELE
LUNGADIGE PORTA VITTORIA
Museo Civico di Storia Naturale
Porta Vittoria
LUNGADIGE GALTROSSA
PONTE NAVI
VIA FILIPPINI
VIA DOGANA
VIA SAN FERMO
VIA LEONI
Porta Leoni
Biblioteca Civica
Chiesa di San Fermo
VIA CAPPELLO
VIA MACELLO
PONTE ALEARDI
Adige
VIA ALEARDI
VIA STELLA
VICO S STELLA
VIA SCALA
Tomba di Giulietta & Museo degli Affreschi
VIA DEL PONTIERE
LUNGADIGE PORTA VITTORIA
VIA CROCE BIANCA
VIA SAN DOMENICO
VIA MONTECCHI
VIA ERBE
VIA PORTICI
VIA CAIROLI
COSTE SCARZARIE
CORSO PORTA BORSARI
EMILEI
VIA EUFEMIA
Porta Borsari
VIA MAZZINI
VIA IV NOVEMBRE
VICOLO S MARCO
VIA STELLA
VIA DIETRO ANFITEATRO
Arena
PIAZZETTA NAVONA
STRADONE S MAFFEI
Palazzo Barbieri
PIAZZA BRA
VIA OBERDAN
VIA DIAZ
VIA CANTORE
CAVOUR
Porta Borsari
VIA S COSIMO
VIA NICCOLO
VIA CATULLO
VIA FRATTA
VIA DISCIPLINA
VIC CHIODO
VIA PALLONE
VIA DIETRO PALLONE
VIA DEGLI ALPINI
Palazzo Gran Guardia
Museo Lapidario Maffeiano
CORSO PORTA NUOVA
VIA MUTILATI
VIA DI SANT'ANTONIO
VIA ROMA
VIC BROSCO
VIA PONTEDORO
Chiesa di San Lorenzo
Arco dei Gavi
VIA SANTO LONGO
PONTE SCALIGERO
Museo di Castelvecchio
Castelvecchio
VIC PONFIDORO
VIC CHIODO
VICOLO MORETTE
VICOLO CIRCOLO
VIA S SILVESTRO
VIA MANIN
CORSO PORTA NUOVA
PIAZZA CITTADELLA
CITTADELLA
VIA S TRINITA
VIA ZAPPATORE
VIA FANTE
VIA DEI FANTE
VIA MONTANARI
VICOLO VOLTO CITTADELLA
VIA BATTISTI
VIA DELLA VALVERDE
VIA TEZONE
VIC TERESE
VIA LANCIERE
VIA SAN TRINITA
VIA TRAINOTTI
VIA DEL CARISTA
VIA MINIATORE
LUNGADIGE CAMPAGNOLA
Arsenale
PIAZZA ARSENALE
PIAZZA ARSENALE
B TRENTO
VIA ARSENALE
LUNGADIGE
CANGRANDE
Adige
VIA PROVOLO
CASTELVECCHIO
STRADONE A PROVOLO
VICOLO DELL'A
VIA MARCONI
VIA DELLA CASA
VIA BERNI FRANCESCO
VIA C SCALZI
VIA GIBERTI
VIA LOCATELLI
VIA PACINOTTO
CIRCONVALLAZIONE
VIA DI NIMES
VIA CITTA
Porta Palio
STR PORTA PALIO
VIA A
VIA SCOPOLI
VIA CAFFI
RIGASTE SAN ZENO
VIA SAN ZENO
SAN ZENO
Basilica di San Zeno
VIA DEL BERSAGLIERE
VIA TOMASO DA VICO
PIAZZA CORLUBBIO
VIA BERTO BARBIANI
PIAZZA POZZA
PIAZZA S ZENO
VICOLO ABBAZIA
VIA LENOTTI
VIA PORTA PALIO
VIA ROSMINI
VIA PORTA SAN ZENO
CIRCONVALLAZIONE PIETRO MARONCELLI
VIALE COLONNELLO GALLIANO
CIRCONVALLAZIONE ALFREDO ORIANI

POI
Cathedral
Information
Police Station
Airport
Railway Stn
Bus Station
Hospital

of the city's history ever since, providing shelter from invading barbarians. ⓐ Piazza Brà ⓣ (045) 800 3204 ⓦ www.arena.it ⓛ 13.45–19.30 Mon, 08.30–19.30 Tues–Sun (last entry 18.45; closes 16.30 on performance days) Ⓝ Bus: 11, 12, 13, 72. Admission charge

Basilica di San Zeno

Most saints depicted in religious art look profoundly bored, uncomfortable, in a trance or downright dour. Not Verona's San Zeno, the African bishop who converted the city to Christianity in the fourth century. The polychrome statue of San Zeno in his church shows him smiling. The frescoes on the walls are freshly cleaned, their colours strong and clear, as is the graffiti inscribed

● *San Zeno is a superb example of Romanesque architecture*

in some of them, autographs of pilgrims and visitors from as far back as the 1600s (look on the wall to the right of the altar, in the frescoes by Veronese). In the lower church, the saint's remains lie in a glass casket. Rebuilt after an earthquake in the early 1100s, San Zeno ranks high as one of the finest examples of Italian Romanesque building to survive. Some of the 48 magnificent bronze panels on the front doors illustrating biblical scenes and the life of San Zeno are older than the present edifice, and legend holds that the Frankish King Pepin, who attended the consecration of the original church in 807, is buried beneath the bell tower. ⓐ Piazza San Zeno ⓘ (045) 592 813 ⓦ www.chieseverona.it ⓛ 08.30–18.00 Mon–Sat, 13.00–18.00 Sun, Mar–Oct; 10.00–13.00, 13.30–17.00 Tues–Sat, 13.00–17.00 Sun, Nov–Feb ⓝ Bus: 31. Admission charge

Castelvecchio & Ponte Scaligero

Cangrande II della Scala built his impressive brick castle on the River Adige between 1355 and 1375 to secure his iron grip on the city after a revolt led by his half-brother. Connecting the castle to the other side of the river is Ponte Scaligero, castellated to make it easier to defend. It stood as one of the world's finest examples of 13th-century engineering, until the night of 25 April 1945, when the retreating German army mined it. Like Ponte Pietra, it was painstakingly rebuilt after the war from the original materials salvaged from the river. To house one of Italy's premier art museums (see page 86), the castle interior was brilliantly redesigned as an art gallery by Venetian architect Carlo Scarpa. Inside this modern gallery is a gathering of northern Italian art that spans the centuries from the Roman and Middle Ages to the 1700s (later works are in the city's other art museum, at Palazzo Forti, see page 69). Works by Gothic and Renaissance painters are particularly strongly represented. The

⬥ *The walls of Castelvecchio*

museum shows works by Stefano da Verona, Mantegna, Pisanello and Tintoretto.

The original equestrian sculpture of Cangrande that used to top the Scaligero Arch above the door of the Chiesa di Santa Maria Antica has been brought here to protect it from the weather and is displayed in a setting designed by Scarpa. So concerned was he to get the setting right for this statue – one of the world's great works of 14th-century sculpture – that he made more than 600 drawings before he completed the platform and surroundings. ⓐ Corso Castelvecchio, at end of Corso Cavour ⓣ (045) 594 734 ⓝ Bus: 21, 22, 23, 24, 31, 32, 33, 41, 61, 62

Chiesa di San Fermo Maggiore

Several surprising treasures hide in this little-visited church near the river, but its newest masterpiece is visible any time. A series of exceptional contemporary bronze panels decorates the front doors. From inside on the right, a doorway leads down to an earlier church, which became the crypt for the present church that the Benedictines began building over in 1070. Frescoes from the seventh and eighth centuries decorate its walls and columns. ⓐ Stradone San Fermo ⓣ (045) 592 813 ⓛ www.chieseverona.it ⓦ 10.00–18.00 Mon–Sat, 13.00–18.00 Sun, Mar–Oct; 10.00–13.00, 13.30–17.00 Tues–Sat, 13.00–17.00 Sun ⓝ Bus: 11, 12, 13, 14, 51, 72, 73. Admission charge

Chiesa di San Lorenzo

Begun in 1110, this Romanesque church is remarkable for its rare women's galleries (few of these survive today, although they were common in churches of the Middle Ages) and for its red marble door, which dates from the Renaissance. ⓐ Corso Cavour ⓣ (045) 592 813 ⓛ 10.00–18.00 Mon–Sat, 13.00–18.00 Sun, Mar–Oct; 10.00–16.00

> **WHAT IS THE TRUE DEFINITION OF 'PALAZZO'?**
> While the Italian *palazzo* sounds like 'palace' in English,
> the word can be used to imply anything from a prestigious
> building to a royal home.

Tues–Sat, 13.30–17.00 Sun, Nov–Feb Bus: 21, 22, 23, 24, 31, 32, 33, 41, 61, 62. Admission charge

Corso Cavour Palazzi

Corso Cavour parallels the river between Castelvecchio and Ponte Vittoria, its relatively short length lined by distinguished palaces of Veronese nobility. The top of Palazzo Canossa, at no. 44, is lined with statues and the current Banca d'Italia building has caryatids on the façade. Palazzo Carlotti, at the corner of Via Diaz, near the Porta Borsari gate, is one of Verona's few late baroque palaces. Bus: 21, 22, 23, 24, 31, 32, 33, 41, 61, 62

Piazza Brà

If Piazza Brà were any smaller, the massive Arena (see page 78) would overwhelm it. But the leafy park in the middle – surrounded by the Palazzo Barbieri (now the municipal building), the older Palazzo Gran Guardia, and a graceful curving line of 19th-century buildings whose stately porticoes and awnings shelter a long arc of cafés – combine to create a balanced and well-used public drawing room for the Veronese. The arched gateway, Portone della Brà (look for the Shakespeare quote, 'there is no world without Verona's walls', carved into its right side) and its octagonal tower are the finishing flourish. Bus: 11, 12, 13, 72

Tomba di Giulietta (Juliet's Tomb)

In the appropriately atmospheric crypt of San Francesco al Corso, an empty stone sarcophagus has been designated as Juliet's. A series of contemporary bronze panels illustrates the story. ⓐ Via Shakespeare, off Via del Pontiere ⓣ (045) 800 0361 ⓛ 08.30–19.30 Tues–Sun, 13.30–19.30 Mon (last entry 18.45). Admission charge

Verona's walls

While Verona's central location on the crossroads of trade routes made it an important city, the same routes that made trade easy also put Verona in the path of invaders. The sharp curve in the river provided some natural defence, but not quite enough, so the Veronese reinforced this natural protection with successive lines of sturdy walls. Still unusually complete for a city of its size, these date from the 12th and 13th centuries. Portone della Brà, at the southern end of Piazza Brà, is the most striking reminder of the early walls. Five 16th-century gates, part of the outer defence system that survives intact around the southern and western sides of the city, make impressive entrances. ⓝ Bus: 11, 12, 13, 72

CULTURE

Amateur artists may enjoy popping into the **Accademia di Belle Arti Cignaroli** (ⓦ www.accademiacignaroli.it), an active art school of painting, sculpture and even fresco painting. Watch tomorrow's maestri at work in the Accademia's *palazzo* on Via Montanarito.

Museo degli Affreschi (Fresco Museum)

You walk through this museum to reach the Tomba di Giulietta (see above), but don't rush past without admiring the collections of beautiful frescoes which once graced the walls of 16th-century Verona. ❷ Via del Pontiere 35 ❶ (045) 800 0361 ❹ 08.30–19.30 Tues–Sun, 13.30–19.30 Mon (last entry 18.45) ⓝ Bus: 11, 12, 13, 72. Admission charge

Museo di Castelvecchio (Castelvecchio Museum)

The Scaligeri Castle, built in the 1300s, was adapted to house the city's remarkable collections of art, dating from the time of the Lombards, through the Middle Ages and into the 19th century (later works are exhibited in the Palazzo Forti branch of the civic museum – see page 69). If you have time to walk through the whole museum, it is a good introduction to the progression of art styles and techniques over almost two millennia. Artists represented here include Bellini, Pisano, Rubens, Tintoretto, Tiepolo and Guardi. It is considered among Italy's best museums. ❷ Corso Castelvecchio 2, inside Castelvecchio (see page 81) ❶ (045) 806 2611 ❹ 13.45–19.30 Mon, 08.30–19.30 Tues–Sun ⓝ Bus: 21, 22, 23, 24, 31, 32, 33, 41, 61, 62. Admission charge

Museo Civico di Storia Naturale (Museum of Natural History)

The Lessina Mountains north and east of Verona are rich in plant and animal fossils and this museum has an outstanding collection of them. ❷ Lungadige Porta Vittoria 9 ❶ (045) 807 9400 ⓦ www.museostorianaturaleverona.it ❹ 09.00–19.00 Mon–Thur & Sat, 14.00–19.00 Sun ⓝ Bus: 73. Admission charge

Museo Lapidario Maffeiano

Stones retrieved from ruins and excavations of Roman Verona form the basis of this collection, and give just a hint of what the city must have looked like 2,000 years ago. Other collections include stonework of the ancient Greeks, Etruscans and others. ❷ Piazza Brà 28

📞 (045) 590 087 🕐 13.30–19.30 Mon, 08.30–19.30 Tues–Sun
(last entry 18.45) 🚍 Bus: 11, 12, 13, 72. Admission charge

RETAIL THERAPY

There are few shops here except for along the streets just
behind the Arena and the everyday shops in the outlying
residential neighbourhoods. The exception is Via Roma, which
runs from Piazza Brà to Castelvecchio, and some smaller streets
in this area. Most of the shops here close all day Sunday and on
Monday morning.

Boutique Novella Hit the street looking like you live here, with trendy
designer rags, accessories and jewellery from Italian makers. 🏠 Via
Carlo Cattaneo 18 📞 (045) 595 670 🕐 15.30–19.30 Mon, 09.30–13.00,
15.30–19.30 Tues–Sat 🚍 Bus: 11, 12, 13, 72

Città del Sole Toys for big kids, as well as little ones, with gadgets,
telescopes, puzzles and hi-tech things in addition to the expected
wooden toys and kiddie stuff. 🏠 Via Carlo Cattaneo 8/B 📞 (045) 591 761
🌐 www.cittadelsole.com 🕐 15.30–10.30 Mon, 09.00–12.30,
15.30–19.30 Tues–Sat 🚍 Bus: 11, 12, 13, 72

Dada The Via Roma area is full of small, hip clothes shops, and this
one has casual styles and comfy things. 🏠 Via Marconi Guglielmo 2
📞 (045) 592 770 🕐 15.00–19.30 Mon, 09.00–19.30 Tues–Sat,
10.00–12.30, 15.00–19.30 Sun 🚍 Bus: 72

Linus The no-leather store: quality high-fashion shoes, bags and
accessories in alternative materials, at good prices, just off Piazza Brà.

🄰 Via Teatro Filarmonico 3 🛈 (045) 801 0922 🆆 www.lescarpedilinus.it
🕒 15.30–19.30 Mon, 09.30–13.00, 15.30–19.30 Tues–Sat (sometimes open Sun) 🄽 Bus: 11, 12, 13, 72

Vibra Hip-hop threads and music to match, for both sexes. Choose a CD, then the clothes and shoes to go with it. 🄰 Via Marconi 10 🛈 (045) 804 1907 🆆 www.vibrarecords.com 🄽 Bus: 11, 12, 13, 72

TAKING A BREAK

Il Gelatone di Piazza Corrubbio £ ❶ Good for a quick pick-me-up after the walk to San Zeno, with plenty of frosty flavours to choose from. 🄰 Piazza Corrubbio 23 🛈 (045) 595 676 🕒 11.30–20.00 Tues–Sun, Feb–Oct & Dec 🄽 Bus: 31

Osteria Retrogusto £ ❷ Cheese and food shop with a small café where you can sample wondrous cheeses from all over Italy, along with other delectable treats, for lunch. 🄰 Via Berni Francesco 1 (at the corner of Via Giberti) 🛈 (045) 800 2167 🕒 Via Berni Francesco 1, corner of Via Giberti 🄽 Bus: 23, 24, 31, 41

Pasticceria Barini £ ❸ Luscious pastries and confections, including delectable little biscuits called Baci di Giulietta (Juliet's kisses), in a classy setting just through Portone della Brà. 🄰 Corso Porta Nuova 8 🛈 (045) 803 0449 🆆 www.pasticceriabarini.it 🕒 06.00–21.00 🄽 Bus: 11, 12, 13, 72

Pizzeria Torre 5 £ ❹ Smart *pizzeria* with whopping salads and generously topped pizzas, also just outside the Portone della Brà

gate. ⓐ Corso Porta Nuova 9 (enter from Via Ghiaia) ❶ (045) 597 832
❶ 12.30–15.00, 19.30–23.00 Ⓝ Bus: 11, 12, 13, 72

La Taverna del Mastino £ ❺ Stop by for excellent *bruschette* or
a glass of wine. ⓐ Stradone San Fermo 17/A ❶ (045) 800 2270
Ⓦ www.tavernadelmastino.com ❶ 19.00–23.30 Ⓝ Bus: 11, 12, 13,
14, 51, 72, 73

AFTER DARK

Piazza Brà and the area between it and Castelvecchio are the hot
districts to visit at night, and across the river, near the university,
are a lot of student hangouts. On a summer evening, be sure to
book ahead or stake out your table early in this area, especially if
you want to sit outdoors.

RESTAURANTS

Al Ristori da Celestino £–££ ❻ Tucked away off Via Manin, this
little *trattoria* serves its own smoked salmon and swordfish, homely
dishes like *pasta e fagioli* and tender veal scallops in saffron cream.
Fixed-price lunches are a bargain. ⓐ Vicolo Valle 1 ❶ (045) 803 1636
❶ 12.30–14.30 Mon, 12.30–14.30, 19.15–22.00 Tues–Sat Ⓝ Bus: 21, 22,
23, 24, 31, 32, 33, 41, 61, 62

La Costa in Brà £–££ ❼ Try ravioli with smoked ricotta and poppy
seeds for a starter. The long pizza menu offers some interesting
toppings. ⓐ Piazza Brà 2 ❶ (045) 597 468 Ⓦ www.lacostainbra.it
❶ 08.00–02.30 June–Sept; 09.00–23.00 Nov–Mar; 08.00–00.00
Apr & May Ⓝ Bus: 11, 12, 13, 72

Osteria da Ugo £–££ ➑ Taste fresh, local, seasonal specialities and wines from the surrounding region at this popular (if slightly touristy) restaurant. It's usually packed full, so book in advance. ⓐ Vicolo Dietro San Andrea 1/B, off Via San Cosimo ➐ (045) 594 400 ⓦ www.osteriadaugo.com ➐ 12.00–14.30, 19.30–22.30 Tues–Sat, 12.00–14.30 Sun ⓝ Bus: 11, 12, 13, 51, 70, 71, 72

Pizzeria No 5 £–££ ➒ In a sleek modern setting of red, white and chrome, this riverside restaurant serves excellent pizza, crispy seafood *fritto misto* (mixed fry) and a creative menu of other dishes. ⓐ Via Macello 5 ➐ (045) 806 5150 ➐ 12.30–14.30, 19.30–22.30 Tues–Sun ⓝ Bus: 31

Rosa Blu £–££ ➓ Pizza from the wood-fired oven is a speciality, but the restaurant is far more than that, with a full kitchen that excels with fish dishes. ⓐ Piazza Corrubbio 29 ➐ (045) 803 6731 ➐ 12.00–15.00, 18.30–00.00 Thur–Tues ⓝ Bus: 31

Osteria Casa Vino ££ ⓫ Begin with their cheese pie with braised leeks or assorted vegetables – it's a speciality of this historic *osteria*. So is the traditional rabbit *cacciatore*. Go for the seasonal specialities, like stuffed courgette flowers. ⓐ Vicolo Morette 8 ➐ (045) 800 4337 ➐ 12.30–14.30, 19.00–22.30 Wed–Mon ⓝ Bus: 21, 22, 23, 24, 31, 32, 33, 41, 61, 62

Enoteca Cangrande ££–£££ ⓬ The constantly changing short menu is a nice mix of traditional and modern (perhaps cannelloni wrapped like crêpes around a filling of *porcini* and truffles with an excellent *fontina* cheese) and the dishes are nicely prepared and artistically served. ⓐ Via Dietro Listone 19/D ➐ (045) 595 022 ➐ 12.15–14.30, 18.00–22.30 Wed–Sun ⓝ Bus: 11, 12, 13, 72

Trattoria Tre Marchetti £££ ⓭ With a façade decorated with fairy lights and bouquets of flowers surrounding the entrance, tiny Trattoria Tre Marchetti has just two lines of tables in its long, thin interior. Be sure to book well in advance, as this spot is very popular with the pre- and post-opera crowd. ⓐ Vicolo Tre Marchetti 19/B, off Via San Nicolò near the Arena ⓣ (045) 803 0463 ⓛ 19.00–22.30 Oct–May; 19.00–05.00 Tues–Sun, June–Sept (for after-show dinners) ⓝ Bus: 11, 12, 13, 72

BARS & CLUBS

Venues are scattered, several of them near San Zeno, with student hangouts in Veronetta, off Via XX Settembre. You can take a bus to these, but you'll have to walk home or take a cab.

Al Mascaron Laid-back cocktail and wine bar with occasional live music. ⓐ Piazza San Zeno 16 ⓣ (045) 597 081 ⓛ 08.00–15.00, 18.00–02.00 ⓝ Bus: 31

Bottega del Krapfen This bakery's opening hours make it ideal for those who need a little bite of something sweet before heading home after a night on the town (it also caters to those on a more conventional schedule). Situated along the river over Ponte Navi, this is a must for doughnut nuts. ⓐ Lung'adige Porta Vittoria 15/B ⓣ (045) 800 4877 ⓛ 23.00–01.00 Mon–Thur, 03.00–05.00 Fri & Sat ⓝ Bus: 11, 12, 13, 14, 51

Bodeguita del Medio Located just of Piazza Brà, this tiny joint serves up killer cocktails. Go during happy hour (18.00–21.00) on Wednesday and Thursday, when drinks are three for the price of two. ⓐ Via Leoncino 35/A ⓣ (340) 383 3708 ⓛ 18.00–03.00 ⓝ Bus: 11, 12, 13, 72

Campus As the name suggests, this place is popular with students from the nearby university who enjoy the long beer list, low prices and plentiful cheap snacks. Billiards and other games are on offer. ⓐ Via XX Settembre 18 ⓣ (045) 800 1549 ⓛ 19.00–02.00 Sun–Thur, 19.00–04.00 Fri & Sat Ⓝ Bus: 11, 12, 13, 51

CINEMAS & THEATRES

Arena di Verona The big venue for top music performances is the Roman Arena, which is also the site of the annual summer opera festival from late June to August. ⓐ Piazza Brà 28 ⓣ (045) 805 1811 ⓦ www.arena.it Ⓝ Bus: 11, 12, 13, 72

Filarmonico The city's oldest cinema house and also its most popular, busy at weekends from early afternoon until the last show at midnight. ⓐ Via Roma 2 ⓣ (045) 596 826 Ⓝ Bus: 21, 22, 23, 24, 31, 32, 33, 41, 61, 62

Fiume Classics and new international cinema releases in this spacious theatre. Films are shown outdoors in the summer. ⓐ Vicolo Cere 14 ⓣ (045) 800 2050 ⓦ www.cinemadiamante.it Ⓝ Bus: 31

Rivoli The latest Hollywood blockbusters hit the big screen here first. ⓐ Piazza Brà 10 ⓣ (045) 590 855 ⓦ www.multisalarivoli.it Ⓝ Bus: 11, 12, 13, 72

▶ *Lake Garda's mild climate attracts vistors year round*

OUT OF TOWN
trips

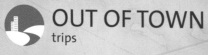

Around Verona

Verona sits between the gentle landscapes of the wide Po River valley and the Lessini Mountains, the steeply rising foothills of the Dolomites. Small villages with hilltop castles, dramatic natural wonders and two of Italy's best-known wine regions – Soave (see page 96) and Valpolicella (see page 101) – are within easy reach.

GETTING THERE

By road

The only way to reach this beautiful area is by road. Although several buses (Ⓦ www.aptv.it) a day run to Montecchio Maggiore, Solferino, Soave and Sant'Ambrogio in Valpolicella, a hire car is the preferred option for getting around, especially to the vineyards, which are often isolated. The following indications can help you to plan day trips, but it's wise to purchase a detailed map of the area before setting out behind the wheel.

Montecchio Maggiore and Soave are both located to the east of Verona, 42 km and 30 km (26 and 19 miles) respectively, along the A4. Solferino, 45 km (28 miles) to the west of of the city and south of Lake Garda, is reached by heading west on the A4. To arrive at Valeggio and Borghetto (approximately 56 km, or 35 miles southwest of Verona), take the A4 to Desenzano, then head south on the SS567, eventually reaching the city on the SP68. The Valpolicella wine region is just a short drive northeast of Verona, around 10–15 km (6–9 miles) along the SS12 from Piazzale Porta Nuova.

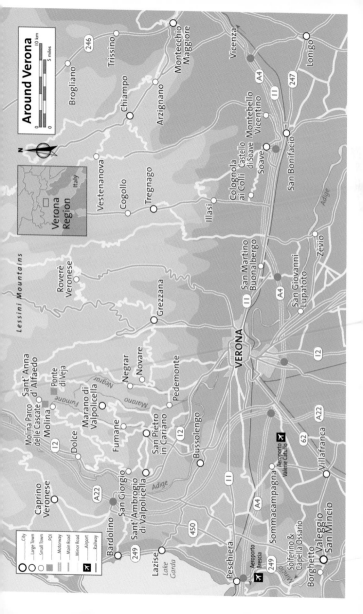

SOAVE

Probably best known for its wine, Soave is also of historical interest in that it's a medieval city that's still completely surrounded by defensive walls.

SIGHTS & ATTRACTIONS
Castello di Soave (Soave Castle)
Built on the site of a Roman fort, the medieval castle dominates Soave, climbing in stages up the hillside behind it. One of its major draws is its horribly claustrophobic dungeon. You can picnic inside the grounds and climb the crenellated walls. ⓐ Via Castelli ❶ (045) 786 0036 ⓦ www.castellodisoave.it ❶ 09.00–12.00, 15.00–18.30 May–Sept; 09.00–12.00, 14.00–16.00 Oct–Dec, Mar & Apr; 09.00–12.00, 14.00–16.00 Sat & Sun, Jan & Feb. Admission charge

RETAIL THERAPY
Soave's main street has several small shops worth browsing, and its market is held on the third Sunday of each month.

TAKING A BREAK
Casablanca Café £ There are cosy booths in the back room, but locals drink their Soave standing at the bar to be closer to the buffet of tasty snacks – *focaccia*, anchovies, marinated olives, meatballs and *peperoncini*. ⓐ Via Roma 27 ❶ (045) 619 0618 ❶ 08.00–21.00

Enoteca Il Drago £ Simple pasta dishes or a plate of salami, cured meats and cheese goes well with a little local wine, sold by the glass so you can sample a variety. A stone's throw from the tourist office.

ⓐ Piazza Antenna 1 ⓣ (045) 768 0670 ⓒ 10.00–15.00, 18.00–01.00 Tues–Sun

ACCOMMODATION

Al Gambero £ Twelve comfortable rooms are inside the walled town, just through its main gate. It has an excellent restaurant.
ⓐ Corso Vittorio Emanuele 5 ⓣ (045) 768 0010
ⓦ www.ristorantealgambero.it

Roxy Plaza Hotel ££ Right in the centre of town, this large hotel is near the castle walls that flow downhill through vineyards. The Old Town and its *enoteche* are an easy walk from the door. ⓐ Via San Matteo 4 ⓣ (045) 619 0660 ⓦ www.hotelroxyplaza.it

SOLFERINO

Ten kilometres (6 miles) south of Lake Garda, the tiny village of Solferino is known for two things: one, for being the site, in 1859, of a massive battle at which Napoleon III helped free the area of Austrian rule (see below); two, for being exquisitely beautiful.

SIGHTS & ATTRACTIONS
Capella Ossario

The staggering casualties on both sides in the Battle of Solferino – more than 40,000 dead or injured – so moved a certain Swiss expat named Henry Dunant that he began a crusade that led to the founding of the International Red Cross. Now the serene and sobering Capella Ossario (in the village's main street) commemorates those of both armies who lost their lives here, its walls lined with skulls and bones

⬤ *The Capella Ossario at Solferino*

of the dead. ☎ (0376) 854 019 ◷ 09.00–12.30, 14.30–18.30 Tues–Sun, mid-May–mid-Oct

RETAIL THERAPY
Solferino's market is on the second Sunday of each month.

AFTER DARK
Pizzeria Al Castello ££ Excellent pizza and a view of Lake Garda from

a hilltop terrace near the Capella Ossario Red Cross monument.
🅐 Piazza Castello 21–22 🅣 (0376) 55 255 🅛 18.30–22.00 Wed–Mon

Ristorante da Renato ££ A bright dining room serving local specialities, such as pumpkin *tortelli* and snails with wild greens. 🅐 Via Ossario 27 🅣 (0376) 854 051 🅦 www.darenato.it 🅛 19.30–21.30

ACCOMMODATION
Hotel Alla Vittoria Da Renato £ This classic family-owned albergo has stood for almost a century. Sit on the front terrace with the locals for a glass of wine in the early evening. 🅐 Via Ossario 27 🅣 (0376) 854 051 🅦 www.darenato.it

VALEGGIO & BORGHETTO

When the local silk industry declined, local women saved Valeggio by opening small restaurants and making pasta. Less than 30 km (20 miles) southwest of Verona, Valeggio soon became a popular place for Veronese to go for dinner. They later restored the nearby abandoned mill village of Borghetto, set picturesquely at a bend in the river: its restaurants, cafés and boutiques come alive at weekends.

SIGHTS & ATTRACTIONS
Castello Scaligero & Parco Giardino Sigurtà
Crossing the Mincio River above Borghetto is a long fortified bridge, Ponte Visconteo, built in 1393, and above it the restored Castello Scaligero, with views all the way to the Dolomite Mountains. You can enter the castle free any time and climb the panoramic castle tower. The beautifully landscaped flower gardens and woodlands of Parco Giardino Sigurtà lie below the castle. Walking is the best way

● *Ruins in the mill village of Borghetto*

to see it, but bicycle hire is available and a tourist train does laps of the park. ☎ (045) 637 1033 ⓦ www.sigurta.it ⓛ 09.00–19.00 Apr–Sept; 09.00–18.00 Oct & Nov (last entry 1 hr before closing)

RETAIL THERAPY
Valeggio's market, which is great for fresh local produce, is held on the fourth Sunday of each month.

AFTER DARK
Ristorante Lepre ££ Just off the main piazza, Lepre is one of the original restaurants that put Valeggio on the culinary map, and it's still a favourite. Dine on *funghi porcini* and peppered beef fillet in the garden in summer. ⓐ Via Marsala 5, Valeggio ☎ (045) 795 0011 ⓛ 12.30–14.30, 19.30–22.00 Fri–Tues, 19.30–22.00 Thur

ACCOMMODATION
Il Borghetto ££ You can rent a self-catering apartment in a renovated water mill dating from 1400, and stay in the little waterside compound of Borghetto after the tourists have gone home for the day. ⓐ Villaggio Vacanze Il Borghetto, Via San Raffaello Sanzio 14/A, Valeggio ☎ (045) 795 2040 ⓦ www.borghetto.it

VALPOLICELLA

This wine region, to the north of Verona, really is grape-tastic. The area enjoys world-wide fame because of its dry Amarone and sweet Recioto wines, with the former in particular vogue at the moment. Little wineries dot the rugged landscape, and villas and their gardens add to the attraction of some of these. If you have a particular interest in wine, this is the one region in the area you should get to know well.

🔺 *Visit the region's vineyards to sample local produce first hand*

WINE TASTINGS IN THE VALPOLICELLA REGION

Visiting the towns and villages of the Valpolicella region and not taking a wine tour would be a missed opportunity: the products are exquisite, the setting sublime and the wine wisdom graciously shared.

Some wineries need a call ahead so they can prepare food to accompany a tasting. Expect to pay for tastings at larger estates, especially those that include food and tours. One of the best wineries to sniff around is **Villa Mosconi-Bertani** (❸ Novare, near Negrar ❶ (045) 602 0744 ❺ 14.00–18.00 Mon, 09.00–13.00, 14.00–18.00 Tues–Fri, 09.00–13.00 Sat). Also in Negrar, the 18th-century **Villa Rizzardi** (❶ (045) 721 0028 ❷ www.guerrieri-rizzardi.it ❺ 15.00–19.00 Thur & Sat, Apr–Oct. Admission charge) is surrounded by the beautiful Italianate and English Gardens of Pojega, created in the late 1700s, with a garden amphitheatre, fountains and waterfalls. Nearby **Casa Vinicola Sartori** offers wine tastings and smaller gardens to tour (❸ Via Casette 2, Negrar ❶ (045) 602 8001). In Pedemonte you can visit the **Tommasi Winery** (❸ Via Ronchetto 2, Pedemonte ❶ (045) 770 1266), an historic estate that has a modern approach to the business of making and selling wine. Look for signs to other wineries that hold tastings or show the winemaking process, all mechanised now.

It is possible to take tours of the Valpolicella wineries from Verona. A nine-hour wine tour typically explores the food, wines and scenery of the region, including at least one full tasting, usually with an English-speaking sommelier. Tours are offered by **Avventure Bellissime** (❶ (041) 520 8616 ❷ www.tours-italy.com) and by **Italy and Wine** (❶ (347) 923 5359 ❷ www.italyandwine.net).

SIGHTS & ATTRACTIONS

Molina Parco delle Cascate (Molina Falls Park)

A large area with nature trails along gorges to several splendid waterfalls, and to caves. This is the kind of place that could almost make you forget the words 'urban' and 'stress'. ⓐ Via Bacilieri ⓣ (045) 772 0185 ⓦ www.cascatemolina.it ⓛ 09.00–19.30, Apr–Sept; 10.00–18.00 Sun only, Mar & Oct. Admission charge

Ponte di Veja

This is Europe's largest natural bridge. It once formed the opening to a cave where artefacts from prehistoric cave dwellers living 100,000 years ago were discovered. The arch is 29 m (95 ft) high, and you can walk across the top. You can see an amazing collection of prehistoric finds and fossils at the **Museo Paleontologico e Preistorico** (ⓐ Piazza dalla Bona ⓛ 09.30–12.30, 15.30–18.30 Tues–Sun, Apr–Oct; 10.00–12.00, 15.00–17.00 Wed, Sat & Sun, Nov–Mar) in nearby Sant'Anna d'Alfaedo.

San Giorgio

One of the prettiest towns in the Valpolicella region is the hilltop San Giorgio, north of Sant'Ambrogio, with a Longobard Romanesque church, Pieve San Giorgio. The tiny cloister beside the church is exquisite, and a little museum has Roman and earlier artefacts.

TAKING A BREAK

Ai Parcheggi £ At the entrance to the waterfall park at Molina, this café/bar is a good place to rest up from the trails. ⓐ Parco delle Cascate, Valpolicella ⓣ (045) 772 0078 ⓛ 09.00–20.30

AFTER DARK

Restaurants

Trattoria da Nicola £ Unfussy local dishes, well prepared. ❸ Via Valle 9, Monte, Sant'Ambrogio di Valpolicella ❶ (045) 776 0180 ❸ 12.00–14.30 Thur–Tues; only open for dinner if pre-booked

Ai Torcoli £–££ A restaurant and pizzeria serving up traditional local specialities with a modern twist. Panoramic views across Valpolicella are terrific. ❸ Via Crocetta 1, Marano di Valpolicella ❶ (045) 680 0609 ❸ 12.00–14.30, 18.30–22.00 Wed–Mon

Ristorante Arquade £££ The chef insists on the freshest local ingredients, treats them royally and serves them artistically. Dining doesn't get any better, and the service matches the food. If you can splash out on only one meal, book it here. ❸ Villa del Quar (see below) ❸ 12.30–14.30, 20.00–22.00 Wed–Sun, 20.00–22.00 Tues, mid–Mar–Dec

ACCOMMODATION

Villa del Quar £££ Staying at this beautifully restored Renaissance villa is one of life's great pleasures. It is in the midst of the classic Valpolicella wine region and has an outstanding wine cellar that includes its own notable wines. The huge outdoor pool is set among the vineyards. ❸ Via Quar 12, Pedemonte ❶ (045) 680 0681 ❸ www.hotelvilladelquar.it ❸ Mid-Mar–Dec

Vicenza

Vicenza's claim to immortality is local-boy-made-good, Andrea Palladio. The clean, graceful lines he brought to the city endure to the 21st century and have inspired structures all over the world. It is the excellent group of Palladian buildings that earned Vicenza its place as a UNESCO World Heritage Site. Despite its beauty, Vicenza is relatively uncrowded and mellow and is an ideal retreat from the crowds of Verona.

South of Vicenza, the Berici Hills rise suddenly. Scenic roads weave and climb through them, revealing little hilltop villages, castles and some outstanding villas. Some of the best of these are now public buildings, so you can see inside.

GETTING THERE

Trains leave Verona's Porta Nuova Station every 30 minutes for Vicenza, a 30-minute ride away, by far the best way to travel in between the two cities.

For bicycle rental in town try **ProntoBici** (❷ Contrada Pedemuro San Biagio 11 ❶ (0444) 526 336). Buses to outlying villages do exist but those visiting countryside vineyards are advised to hire a car.

SIGHTS & ATTRACTIONS

Basilica di Monte Berico

Overlooking the city from the south, the lofty Basilica di Monte Berico was begun in the 15th century in thanksgiving for Vicenza's deliverance from the plague. Now a major pilgrimage site, the ornate interior glows with votive candles. It is home to Montagna's

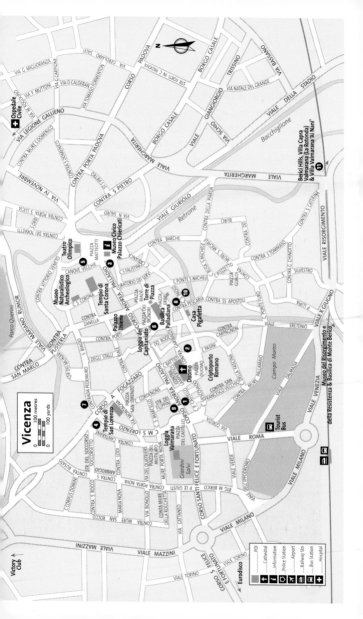

THE VICENZA CARD
The €8 Vicenza Card grants admission to most of the major sights for three days, including Teatro Olimpico and the museums. Cards can be bought at the **tourist office** (ⓐ Piazza Matteotti 12 ⓣ (0444) 320 854 ⓦ www.vicenzae.org), next to the Teatro Olimpico.

Pietà fresco and an unusual collection of needleworked ex votos in a room behind the sanctuary. Veronese's expertly restored *The Supper of Gregory the Great* hangs in the refectory. 🟢 Viale X Giugno 87 🛈 (0444) 326 464 🌐 www.monteberico.it 🕐 06.00–12.30, 14.30–18.00 Mon–Sat (until 19.30 Apr–Oct), 06.00–19.00 Sun 🚍 Bus: 18 (Sun only)

🔻 *View of Vicenza from Piazzale della Vittoria, Monte Berico*

Corso Andrea Palladio

Along this backbone of Vicenza are elegant palaces designed by the great names in architecture. The street begins at Piazza del Castello, with Palladio's Palazzo Bonin (step into the courtyard to see the interior double *loggia*). Palazzo Pojana is close to the centre, on the right, easy to recognise by the gate that allows a street to pass through its centre. Palazzo Thiene, on the left, is so large that it has several façades facing onto different streets. At the far end, a fourth *palazzo* by Palladio is now the Museo Civico (see page 114).

Duomo (Cathedral)

The damage of World War II has been so skilfully repaired that the cathedral, founded in the ninth century, doesn't show the scars. The dome, by Palladio (he rarely worked on churches), has been reconstructed, along with the Gothic façade, which is more than a century older. ⊙ Piazza Duomo ⊙ (0444) 325 007 ⊙ 10.30–11.45, 15.30–18.00 Mon–Sat, 15.30–17.15, 18.00–19.15 Sun

Giardino Salvi & Loggia Valmarana

Just outside the Porta Castello, with its tower acting as a backdrop to its statuary, is a small park with waterside walkways. Crossing the two branches of a stream are two *loggias*, one designed by a follower of Palladio and included on the UNESCO list.

Piazza dei Signori & Basilica Palladiana

A huge statue of Palladio contemplates his work in front of the Basilica Palladiana, also known as the Palazzo della Ragione.

⊙ *The clocktower of the Basilica Palladiana in the Piazza dei Signori*

Overlooking this beautiful piazza from a greater height is the slender Torre di Piazza, which has grown over the centuries to its present 82 m (269 ft). Opposite, the Loggia del Capitaniato is an arcade designed by Palladio. Tuesday mornings and all day Thursday are market days, when the entire square is filled with stalls.

Teatro Olimpico

The last – and to many the greatest – of Palladio's works remained unfinished when he died, but was completed by his prize student, Vincenzo Scamozzi. Dating from 1589, it is Europe's oldest indoor theatre, designed to feel like a Greek open-air amphitheatre. The stage is a masterpiece of theatrical illusion; it's hard to tell where stage sets end and the painted backdrop begins. ⓐ Piazza Matteotti 11 ① (0444) 222 800 ⓛ 09.00–16.30 Tues–Sun. Admission charge

Tempio di San Lorenzo

The Franciscans built the church early in the Middle Ages, and its interior was decorated a few centuries later. Above the front portal is an especially beautiful and detailed nativity scene. ⓐ Piazza San Lorenzo 4 ① (0444) 321 960 ⓛ 10.30–12.00, 15.30–19.00 (16.00–19.00 in summer)

Tempio di Santa Corona

The Gothic church was built in the 13th century to house a thorn from Christ's Crown of Thorns, which you can see annually on Good Friday. The church is undergoing restoration work – call the tourist office (see page 108) for an update. The church's former convent is now home to the Museo Naturalistico Archeologico (see page 114). ⓐ Contrada Santa Corona

Villa Capra Valmarana ('La Rotonda')

Palladio's best-known single work is recognised by Americans as the model for Thomas Jefferson's home at Montecello, and was itself based on the Pantheon in Rome. ⓐ Via Rotonda 45 ⓣ (0444) 321 793 ⓛ Grounds: 10.00–12.00, 15.00–18.00 Tues–Sun; house open Wed only

Villa Valmarana

Often called Villa ai Nani (Villa of the Dwarfs) after the line of stubby statues that stand atop its wall, Villa Valmarana is worth seeing for its interior: the rooms are decorated with an extraordinary cycle of

▲ *Palladio's exquisite Villa Valmarana ai Nani*

18th-century frescoes by Tiepolo.  Via dei Nani 8 (0444) 321 803 www.villavalmarana.com 10.00–12.00, 15.00–18.00 Tues–Sun, Mar–Oct; 10.00–12.00, 14.00–16.30 Sat & Sun, Nov–Feb Bus: 8 (walk from Villa Rotunda). Admission charge

CULTURE

Museo Civico

Opposite Teatro Olimpico is one of Palladio's grandest city palaces, Palazzo Chiericati, which holds the city's art collection, including works by Bellini, Tiepolo, Montagna and Veronese. Carpione's magnificent frescoed ceiling is near the entrance. Piazza Matteotti 37 (0444) 222 811 www.museicivicivicenza.it 09.00–17.00 Tues–Sun. Admission charge

Museo Naturalistico Archeologico

The natural life of the Berici Hills is explored here, along with prehistoric and ancient finds from the area. Contrà San Corona 4 (0444) 222 815 www.museicivicivicenza.it 09.00–17.00 Tues–Sat (until 19.00 July & Aug). Admission charge

Museo del Risorgimento e della Resistenza

In an art nouveau villa that was headquarters for the Resistance movement, the history of Italy's struggle for independence and unity is shown in an interesting mix of artefacts, photographs and art. Below the museum is a wooded park with walking trails that lead to Villa Rotunda. Viale X Giugno 115, Monte Berico (0444) 322 998 www.museicivicivicenza.it 09.00–13.00, 14.15–17.00 Tues–Sun. Admission charge

RETAIL THERAPY

Vicenza has been a gold capital for centuries, and you'll find small goldsmith's shops tucked under the arcades around Piazza dei Signori and along Corso Andrea Palladio. The entire central city is filled with market stalls on Tuesday morning and all day Thursday.

Casaelmy Beautifully presented silverware, photo frames and charming knick-knacks. ⓐ Contrada Pedemuro San Biagio ⓣ (0444) 322 813 ⓛ 09.30–12.30, 16.00–19.30 Tues–Sun, 16.00–19.30 Mon

⬤ *Bargain-hunters search the market stalls*

Euroart Continuing the fine Vicenza art of gold-smithing, this little shop designs and creates elegant jewellery, including tiny gold picture frames to wear. ⓐ Contrà Generale Chinotto 6 ❶ (0444) 525 222 ⓦ www.euroart.it ❶ 10.00–12.30, 15.00–18.00 Tues–Sat

Mercatini Antiquariato From March to December the region's antique dealers hold a large antiques market in the Piazza dei Signori on the second Sunday of the month. ❶ (0444) 323 863

TAKING A BREAK

Antico Bar del Corso £ ❶ The cosy café is under the vaulting, with an airy little outdoor café in a courtyard and good sandwiches. ⓐ Corso Andrea Palladio 54 ❶ (0444) 525 336 ❶ 07.00–20.30 Sun–Thur, 07.00–22.30 Fri & Sat

Antico Café Scrigni £ ❷ Locals have been sipping espresso and munching cakes here since 1860. ⓐ Piazza Duomo 1 ❶ (0444) 324 920 ❶ 07.30–00.00

Caffè £ ❸ Cosy cafe with outdoor tables, perfectly placed by the tourist office and Teatro Olimpico. ⓐ Piazza Matteotti 4 ❶ (0444) 389 010 ❶ 07.00–02.00 Tues–Sun

Fogazzaro £ ❹ A great deli and café serving *bruschette* and other savoury snacks. ⓐ Corso Antonio Fogazzaro 85 ❶ (0444) 321 430 ❶ 07.30–21.00 Tues–Sun

Nirvana Caffè degli Artisti £ ❺ Cakes and *panini* (grilled vegetable *panini* is fresh and delicious) served at tables inside

⬤ Try the local dishes in one of the many restaurants

or under the arched portico beside Teatro Olimpico. ⓐ Piazza Matteotti 8 ⓘ (0444) 543 111 ⓛ 08.00–20.00 Sun–Thur, 08.00–23.30 Fri & Sat

Gran Caffè Garibaldi ££ ⑥ Beside the Loggia del Capitaniato, the raised terrace of the Garibaldi is not only the place to be seen, but also provides the best view of the evening groovers. In bad weather, retreat to the elegant interior. ⓐ Via Cavour 7 (Piazza dei Signori) ⓘ (0444) 544 147 ⓛ 08.00–01.00 Wed–Sun (hours vary)

AFTER DARK

Vicenza has a surprisingly active nightlife for a city of its size. Both the tourist office and several cafés and bars have shelves full of flyers on both concert/theatre schedules and the bar/disco scene.

RESTAURANTS

Antico Guelfo £ ⑦ An elegant, recently restored *osteria* – especially good for travellers with food intolerances or allergies. ⓐ Contrada Pedemuro San Biagio 92 ⓘ (0444) 547 897 ⓦ www.anticoguelfo.it ⓛ 19.00–23.00 Mon–Sat

Antica Osteria al Bersagliere ££ ⑧ A few doors downhill from Piazza Erbe. Cream sauces, mushrooms and hearty *ragoûts* complement the perfectly formed wine list ⓐ Contrà Pescaria 11 ⓘ (0444) 323 507 ⓛ 12.00–14.30, 19.30–22.30 Tues–Sat, 12.00–14.30 Sun

Antica Trattoria Tre Visi ££ ⑨ Step through the arched portico of a former *palazzo* to find this venerable restaurant. ⓐ Corso Andrea Palladio 25 ⓘ (0444) 324 868 ⓛ 12.30–14.30, 17.30–23.00 Tues–Sun

Osteria I Monelli ££ ⑩ Traditional local dishes served in a warm, inviting rustic atmosphere. It is open later than most restaurants.
ⓐ Contrà Ponte San Paolo 13 ① (0444) 540 400 ⓛ 11.30–15.00, 18.30–01.00

Villa Michelangelo ££–£££ ⑪ The chef is up to the setting – the *agnolotti* are simply the finest on earth. If you don't have a car, the dining experience is well worth the taxi ride from the city centre.
ⓐ Via Sacco 35, Arcugnano ① (0444) 550 300 ⓛ 12.30–14.00, 20.00–22.00

◐ *The restaurant at Villa Michelangelo is one of the finest in the region*

BARS & CLUBS

Art Café This young and trendy bar spills onto 20 tables in the Piazza San Lorenzo from April until October. ⓐ Corso Antonio Fogazzaro 52 ⓣ (0444) 321 047 ⓛ 14.00–02.00 Tues–Sun

Eno's Uber-chic Eno's has 100 bottles of fine wine behind an electronic sideboard. Put in your credit card and pour yourself a Valpolicella or Soave from €1.50 to €15 per glass. ⓐ Contrà Pescherie Vecchie 16 ⓣ (0444) 913 377 ⓦ www.enosclub.com ⓛ 17.00–01.00

Eurodisco One of the most popular places in town, with some well-known DJs spinning on summer weekends. ⓐ Via Commercio 24 ⓣ (0444) 348 128 ⓛ 12.00–03.00 Tues–Sun

Palladium Disco With a good-sized dance floor, the Palladium's emphasis is on DJs and electronic music. A classy *pizzeria* is a useful addition. ⓐ Via G Marconi 119, Torri di Quartesolo ⓣ (0444) 583 577 ⓦ www.palladium-italy.com ⓛ 18.00–02.00 Wed–Sun

Sartea A popular student haunt, particularly in summer months when the partying takes place in a lovely garden. ⓐ Corso Santi Felice e Fortunato 372 ⓣ (0444) 563 725 ⓛ 10.00–02.00 Tues–Sun

Victory A classy setting, with live acts and DJs. A very trendy option so dress to impress. ⓐ Via Biron di Sopra 68/70 ⓣ (0444) 961 499 ⓦ www.victoryclub.it ⓛ 20.00–02.00 Fri & Sat

ACCOMMODATION

Albergo Due Mori £ Effortlessy chic but without the usual price or attitude that accompanies cool. From the parquet floors and antique radiators in the foyer to the 30 guestrooms, this is a really graceful, not to mention quiet, option. ➌ Contrà Do Rode 24–26 ➊ (0444) 321 886 Ⓦ www.hotelduemori.com

Hotel Castello ££ Hidden in the maze of quiet streets west of the Piazza Erbe. Converted from a 19th-century inn this trendy haven of peace also has a rooftop terrace with fine views. ➌ Contrà Piazza del Castello 24 ➊ (0444) 231 485 Ⓦ www.hotelcastelloitaly.it

Hotel Doge ££ This beautifully appointed modern hotel offers secure covered parking and a pretty garden, a ten-minute walk from Vicenza's historic centre. ➌ Via Lamamora 20 ➊ (0444) 923 616 Ⓦ www.hoteldoge-vi.it

Hotel Cristina ££–£££ The Cristina's claim to fame is that it is an environmentally friendly hotel. It is also very pleasant, with pretty, themed rooms. ➌ Corso Santi Felice e Fortunato 32 ➊ (0444) 323 751 Ⓦ www.hotelcristinavicenza.it

Hotel Villa Michelangelo £££ Grace and elegance are the hallmarks of this hilltop villa. The rooms are luxurious without being pompous, and a swimming pool makes this a nice place to escape the summer heat of the valley. Weddings are a speciality, and you couldn't find a more romantic spot. ➌ Via Sacco 35, Arcugnano ➊ (0444) 550 300 Ⓦ www.hotelvillamichelangelo.com

Lake Garda

When the summer heat turns the city into a sauna, everyone who can heads to the lake at weekends and in the evening, jostling for space with the Germans who arrive through the Brenner Pass.

GETTING THERE

The hubs of Peschiera and Desenzano del Garda are both connected by rail to Verona's Porta Nuova Station. Trains take around 20 or 30 minutes respectively, and leave every 30 minutes.

Buses leave for Garda, Bardolino, Salò, Sirmione and most other places around the lake from the bus station outside Porta Nuova. Regular buses also circle the lake between towns such as Riva del Garda and Desenzano.

For mountain bike rental and excursions try **Bike Shope Xtreme** (🅐 Via Navene Vecchia 10, Malcesine 🅣 (045) 740 0105) below the *funivia* (cable car) station (see page 128).

Gestione Navigazione Laghi runs several routes on the lake including the run from Desenzano in the south to Riva on the northern shore stopping at Sirmione, Peschiera, Bardolino and Gardone (🅣 800 551 801 🅦 www.navigazionelaghi.it). Also popular is the east to west cross-lake run from Torri del Bénaco to Maderno.

SIGHTS & ATTRACTIONS

Bardolino

Bardolino spreads along the shore in what seems like one long piazza, with the water on one side and café umbrellas on the other. Worth seeking out are the ninth-century Carolingian San Zeno and the

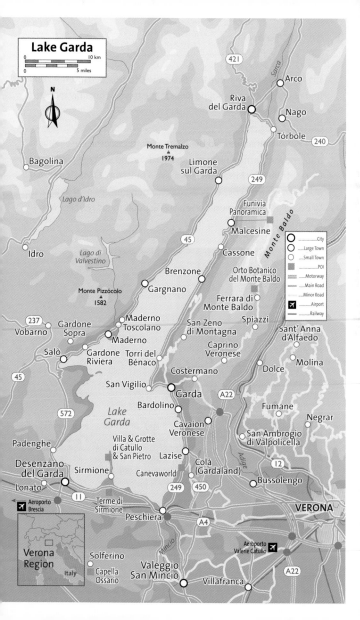

11th-century Romanesque San Severo, with a frescoed interior. You'll find plenty of local Bardolino wine at the town's Thursday market.

Castello Scaligero

This is where Italians held the German writer Goethe prisoner as a spy; now it forms a picturesque backdrop and vantage point for views of the lake. Inside, there is a small museum. ❷ Via Borre, Malcesine ❶ (045) 657 0333 ❿ www.comunemalcesine.it ❶ 09.00–19.00 Apr–Oct; 09.00–19.00 Sat, Sun & public holidays, Nov–Mar. Admission charge

Desenzano del Garda & Villa Romana

Decentius, a Roman nobleman, gave his name to this pretty port town and also left behind the ruins of his palatial villa, covered by a mudslide and only unearthed in 1921. Villa Romana has beautiful geometric and figural mosaics, most still in place as they were found. ⓐ Via Crocefisso 22 ⓣ (030) 914 3547 ⓛ 08.30–19.00 Tues–Sat, 09.00–17.30 Sun, Mar–mid-Oct; 08.30–16.30 Tues–Sat, 09.00–16.30 Sun, mid-Oct–Feb. Admission charge

⬇ *The attractive harbour at Desenzano*

◆ *Stunning lake views from Gardone Riviera*

Gardone Riviera & Giardino Botanico André Heller

Climbing the hillside above Gardone, the André Heller Botanic Garden has exotic plants from all continents, an artificial lake and modern sculptures. ❸ Via Roma (S45), Gardone Riviera ❶ (033) 641 0877 ⓦ www.hellergarden.com ⏱ 09.00–19.00 Mar–Oct. Admission charge

CANEVAWORLD

You can keep your suave theme parks with their film-lot reconstructions, out of work actors mincing about in cartoon-character attire and plates of chips at prices that send your credit account into meltdown; it might not be flash, but you get much more bounce to the ounce at Canevaworld. Towards Verona from Gardaland and refreshingly uncutting-edge – one of the attractions in its Movieland area is called 'Blues Brothers 2000' – this tick-all-the-boxes theme park is loads of fun. You'll have a splashing time in Aquaparadise, while the Medieval Times sector is joust the ticket, not least because here you can tuck into King Adolfo's Feast, which includes 'Ruritania Soup'. If that were not alluring enough, the Rock Star Restaurant has an all-you-can eat menu, which is the kind of challenge to which any sophisticated visitor would surely rise. The rides don't threaten the sound barrier, so there are no worries about the grosser manifestations of motion sickness or displaying pure, untrammelled fear in front of the little ones. Queues are rarely so large as to be off-putting. ❸ A22, Verona Nord exit ❶ (045) 696 9900 ⓦ www.canevaworld.it ⏱ Apr–Sept; Oct weekends only; hours vary with the area of the theme park ⓝ Free shuttle buses from Peschiera rail station. Admission charge

Lazise

The enclosed harbour, which has a Venetian customs station at one side of it, is one of the most picturesque on the lake, with an 11th-century castle, once a Scaligeri stronghold, as a backdrop. The 12th-century Church of San Nicolo near the port has a 16th-century bell tower.

Malcesine

Most of Garda's towns sit at lake level, but Malcesine's oldest stone buildings cluster around its fortress, on a craggy cliff. From the castle, wander down Via Borre to the Porte Vecchio with its cafés and unique turtle statue, then along Via Capitanato to the boat harbour, where the lake steamers dock. Malcesine is a favourite for tourists, with its steep, narrow streets and abundance of boutiques and restaurants. **Cable cars** (❶ (045) 740 0206 ⓦ www.funiviedelbaldo.it ❷ 08.00–18.00) run up the hill to Monte Baldo. Rising 1,600 m (5,250 ft) in about ten minutes, the gondolas turn during the second stage, so all passengers can enjoy the spectacular views.

Orto Botanico del Monte Baldo

On top of the spine of Monte Baldo, at the end of a long and dizzying road, the high-altitude garden displays native plants, including edelweiss, wild roses and alpine lilies. ❸ Ferrara di Monte Baldo (above Garda) ❶ (045) 624 7288 ⓦ www.ortobotanicomontebaldo.org ❷ 09.00–18.00 May–Sept

---

● *Lazise's small boat harbour and Venetian customs station*

Parco Termale del Garda

The woods and gardens around the 18th-century Villa Cedri are ideal for strolling and picnicking. There is also a large thermal lake, thermal grotto and a modern spa. Entry to the beautiful park for a day of lounging is good value. ⓐ Piazza di Sopra 4, Colà di Lazise ⓣ (045) 759 0988 ⓦ www.villadeicedri.com ⓛ 10.00–21.00 Mon–Thur, 10.00–02.00 Fri & Sat, 10.00–23.00 Sun. Admission charge

Peschiera & Gardaland

Peschiera is a popular gateway to Lake Garda, and home to its most popular attraction, **Gardaland** (ⓐ S249, Peschiera ⓣ (045) 644 9777 ⓦ www.gardaland.it ⓛ 10.00–18.00 Apr–mid-June, mid-Sept–early Oct; 10.00–23.00 mid-June–mid-Sept; 10.00–18.00 Sat, Sun & holidays, rest of year ⓘ Times vary, so call to check), Italy's biggest theme park. However, be warned: even in the spring and autumn, the traffic along S11 and S572, the roads closest to the lake, can be bumper-to-bumper at the weekend.

Salò

Salò sits at the water's edge under the towering Monte San Bartolomeo. In the central lakeside plaza, the arcades of the Loggia della Magnifica Patria are all that remain of the 16th-century Captain's Palace. The 1453 Duomo, Santa Maria Annunziata, was never finished outside. The Gothic interior makes up for it. Works by Veronese and several other Italian masters are also in the church. One of the largest of the lake towns, Salò has interesting streets, shops, restaurants and cafés.

ⓞ *Malcesine's fortress tops a craggy cliff*

Sirmione

At the end of a peninsula, this town of narrow, shop-lined streets
is almost completely surrounded by water. A medieval castle, Rocca
Scaligeri (they were everywhere), still guards the entrance to the
town with a narrow drawbridge. No cars are allowed inside (unless
you have a hotel reservation there); parking outside the gate fills
early in the summer or at weekends. Inside the little moated castle
is the **Museo del Castello** (① (030) 916 468). Past the shops is the
Chiesa di San Pietro in Mavino, built by the Longobards and rebuilt
in 1300, although its campanile dates from 1070. Inside, frescoes
from the 12th to the 16th centuries are preserved.

Terme di Sirmione

The thermal waters attracted the Romans to Sirmione and still
draw visitors. Since 1889 the waters of a thermal spring have been
used for bathing, and modern spas have added other refinements.
ⓐ Grand Hotel Terme ① (030) 990 4922 Ⓦ www.termedisirmione.com
🕐 07.00–19.00 Apr–Oct; 07.00–13.00 Mon–Sat, Nov–Mar. Admission
charge

Torri del Bénaco & Museo del Castello Scaligero

From this attractive town the lake's only car ferry takes cars back and
forth to Maderno on the western shore. In the centre of town near
the pretty boat harbour, a 13th-century castle houses the **Museo
del Castello Scaligero** (ⓐ Viale Fratelli Lavanda 2 ① (045) 629 6111
Ⓦ www.museodelcastelloditorridelbenaco.it 🕐 09.30–13.00,
16.30–19.30 June–Sept; 09.30–12.30, 14.30–18.00 Apr, May & Oct).
The church of Santissima Trinità has 14th-century frescoes, and
nearby Torre di Berengario dates from the tenth century.

Il Vittoriale degli Italiani

The art deco estate was designed for the Italian author, poet, soldier and adventurer, Gabriele d'Annunzio. The mansion is stuffed with priceless art and historic objects; the grounds contain a huge mausoleum and a sizeable portion of the warship *Puglia*, alongside other curiosities. ❸ Via Vittoriale, Gardone Riviera ❶ (036) 529 6511 ⓦ www.vittoriale.it ❷ 08.30–20.00 Apr–Sept; 09.00–17.00 Oct–Mar. Admission charge

CULTURE

Museo Archeologico Rambotti

Roman artefacts and items from the Palaeolithic, Mesolithic, Neolithic and Bronze Ages form the collections of this small (but very interesting) museum. ❸ Via T Dal Molin 7/C, Desenzano del Garda ❶ (030) 914 4529 ❷ 15.00–19.00 Tues, Sun & holidays

Museo dell'Olio d'Oliva

Olive trees thrive in the temperate climate around the lake, creating an important local industry. This museum tells the story of oil production, and you can sample and buy the results. ❸ Via Peschiera 54 (S249), Cisano di Bardolino ❶ (045) 622 9047 ⓦ www.museum.it ❷ 09.00–12.30, 14.30–19.00 Mon–Sat, 09.00–12.30 Sun (closed Sun in Jan & Feb) ❶ Closed 3 wks in Jan

Museo del Vino

The Zeni Winery's little museum shows the process by which Garda table wines are produced. There are tastings between mid-March and October, and evening tastings by reservation.

🅐 Via Costabella 9, Bardolino ☎ (045) 622 8331 🆆 www.museodelvino.it
🕐 09.00–13.00, 14.00–19.00 (until 18.00 Sat & Sun) mid-Mar–Oct

RETAIL THERAPY

Desenzano and Salò are perhaps the best towns for shopping, but Malcesine has a number of craftsmen's studios and small shops, while Sirmione's streets are lined with the high-end designer and antiquarian shops.

Markets are a regular feature, and you'll find one somewhere nearly every day including Bardolino on Thursday, Garda on Friday and Malcesine on Saturday. Look for art shows and craft fairs in lake towns, especially at weekends.

Casa Bella Martinelli Take back the latest gizmo from classy Lombardy kitchenware designers Alessi. 🅐 Via Pozzo dell'Amore 50, Cavaion Veronese (off the 450 motorway, east of Bardolino) ☎ (045) 626 0344 🆆 www.casabellamartinelli.it 🕐 09.00–12.30, 15.30–19.30 Tues–Sat, 15.30–19.30 Mon

Garda Frutta The shop sells local gastronomic delights including *grappa*, local olive oils and DOC wines from the region. 🅐 Via Verona 174, Lugana di Sirmione (opposite Santa Maria church) ☎ (030) 990 5197 🆆 www.martellifood.it 🕐 08.30–13.00, 16.00–20.00 Tues–Sun, Apr–Oct; 08.30–12.30, 16.00–19.30 Tues–Sat, Nov–Mar

TAKING A BREAK

You won't want for places to sit along the lake and enjoy a *prosecco* or cappuccino, since every town's waterfront is lined with café umbrellas.

Bar Al Porto £ The best-located café tables in Lazise, right on the corner of the lake-shore promenade and the charming boat harbour, at the point where the NaviGarda lake steamers dock. ❷ Piazzale Porto 3, Lazise ❶ (045) 758 0538 ❸ 08.00–20.00

Bar Pasticceria Bosio £ Not only the oldest, but the best pastry café in town, this one specialises in traditional local cakes. ❷ Piazza Malvezzi 5, Desenzano del Garda ❶ (030) 914 2330 ❸ 08.00–01.00 summer; 08.00–20.00 Fri–Wed, winter

Pizzeria La Strambata £ Leave the crowded lake shore to join locals for pizza or enormous *salade caprese*. ❷ Via Fosse, Bardolino ❶ (045) 721 0110 ❸ 12.00–15.00, 18.00–00.00 Thur–Tues

AFTER DARK

The liveliest towns for nightlife tend to be on the southern and eastern shores: Desenzano, Garda, Bardolino and Lazise. Look to Salò, Gardone Riviera and Sirmione for more high-class entertainment aimed at a slightly older age group.

RESTAURANTS
Ristorante Osteria dell'Orologio £ Dishes and wines from around the lake in the historic centre of Salò. ❷ Via Butturini 26, Salò ❶ (036) 529 0158 ❸ 12.00–14.00, 19.00–22.00

Osteria alla Rosa £–££ All the pasta is made right on the premises, and has been for a century. Polenta with sausages and fresh lake fish also available. ❷ Piazza Bocchera 5, off Via Cerche, Malcesine ❶ (045) 657 0783 ❸ 09.00–02.00

Trattoria Riolet ££ Family-run with a lake terrace. Try grilled fish fresh from the lake. ❷ Via Fasano Sopra 75, Gardone Riviera ❶ (036) 520 545 ● 12.00–14.00, 19.00–21.30 Thur–Tues

Agli Angeli ££–£££ Pay a visit for an exceptional dinner, with professional (but friendly) service and artistically presented dishes. ❷ Piazza Garibaldi 2, Gardone Sopra ❶ (036) 520 832 ⓦ www.agliangeli.com ● 12.00–14.00, 20.00–23.00 Tues–Sun

BARS & CLUBS

Taverna Fregoso You can have dinner or pizza here, but most go for the wine and the live music every night (21.00–02.00) in the summer. ❷ Corso Vittorio Emanuele 37, Garda ❶ (045) 725 6622 ● Thur–Tues

Taverna Goethe Locanda This lively (make that raucous, at night) spot is a perennial fave for a glass of wine and often live music. ❷ Via delle Viole 10, Garda ❶ (045) 725 6397 ● 18.00–03.00

ACCOMMODATION

Hotel Roma £ Bargain basement but efficient, friendly and spotlessly clean. All rooms have terraces or balconies on the lake front. Parking available. ❷ Lungolago Regina Adelaide 26, Garda ❶ (045) 725 5025 ⓦ www.hotelromagarda.it ● Mar–Oct

Color Hotel £–££ Famed for its service and sea views, the Color comes with a heated pool, to-die-for toiletries and very contemporary

◀ *Al fresco dining in Malcesine*

furnishings. ❸ Via S. Cristina 5, Bardolino ❶ (045) 621 0857
Ⓦ www.colorhotel.it ❶ Apr–Oct

Hotel Garnì Diana £–££ Inexpensive and charming. Guestrooms
all have balconies with views of the lake or Monte Baldo. Outdoor
swimming pool. ❸ Via Scoisse 8, Malcesine ❶ (045) 750 0192
Ⓦ www.dianamalcesine.com ❶ Apr–mid-Oct

Hotel Vittorio ££ A beautiful example of Italian art deco on the lake
shore. Almost every room has a lake or harbour view: ask for corner
room 410 for the best of both. ❸ Via Porto Vecchio 4, Desenzano
❶ (030) 991 2245 Ⓦ www.hotelvittorio.it ❶ Mar–Nov

Villa Del Sogno £££ Elegant and overlooking the lake, with gardens
surrounding the art deco building, whose central terrace is like
a small private piazza. ❸ Via Zanardelli 107, Gardone Riviera
❶ (036) 529 0181 Ⓦ www.villadelsogno.it ❶ Apr–Oct

● *Take time to explore Verona and the surrounding towns*

PRACTICAL
information

Directory

GETTING THERE

By air

From the UK and Europe several European airlines fly into Verona's Valerio Catullo Airport (see page 46) in Villafranca, about 12 km (7½ miles) southwest of the centre, including **British Airways** (W www.ba.com) from London Gatwick. Low-cost carrier **Ryanair** (W www.ryanair.com) flies from London's Stansted Airport to Aeroporto di Brescia (see page 47), just west of Lake Garda, 60 km (40 miles) west of Verona. **easyJet** (W wwww.easyjet.com) serves Venice's **Marco Polo Airport** (W www.veniceairport.it), although note that this is over 100 km (60 miles) away.

Milan's **Malpensa Airport** (W www.sea-aeroportimilano.it) is northern Italy's major air hub for those arriving from both inside and outside Europe. Verona is a 90-minute train ride from Milan's Stazione Centrale, which is easily reached from the airport via a paying shuttle bus that waits directly outside the arrivals hall.

From North America there are direct flights from New York's JFK to Milan Malpensa Airport on **Alitalia** (W www.alitalia.com) and **Delta** (W www.delta.com), with a New York Newark route on **Continental** (W www.continental.com). Delta also flies from JFK and Philadelphia to Venice's Marco Polo Airport.

Many people are aware that air travel emits CO_2, which contributes to climate change. You may be interested in the possibility of lessening the environmental impact of your flight through **Climate Care** (W www.climatecare.org), which offsets your CO_2 by funding environmental projects around the world.

● *Cruising on Lake Garda*

By rail

To get from London to Verona by rail, take the Eurostar from London St Pancras International Station to Paris, then change for Milan's Stazione Centrale. On fast trains, the trip takes around ten hours, but on cheaper, slower trains it will take you longer. From Milan, it takes around 90 minutes to get to Verona. You can also take a train direct from Paris to Verona, but depending on timetables it may be quicker to go via Milan. Within Italy, be sure to validate your ticket at one of the yellow machines on the platform before boarding. For timetables and more information on Italian trains, contact **Trenitalia** (☎ 892 021 (within Italy) ⓦ www.trenitalia.it).

There are various multi-day national and international train passes available. Check the following websites and publications:
Rail Europe A one-stop source of information, reservations and tickets, including Eurostar. ☎ +44 8448 484 064 ⓦ www.raileurope.co.uk
Thomas Cook European Rail Timetable Up-to-date train timetables in Europe. ☎ +44 1733 416 477 ⓦ www.thomascookpublishing.com
The Man in Seat Sixty-One International rail travel advice and information. ⓦ www.seat61.com

By road

The quickest way from London to Verona is via Reims and Basle along the E50, E25 and E35. This 1250 km- (800 mile-) trip should take around 13 hours. In Italy, as in the rest of the continent, driving is on the right-hand side of the road.

Cheaper than flying and less tiring than driving is the coach journey from London Victoria to Milan on **Eurolines** (☎ +44 871 781 8181 ⓦ www.eurolines.co.uk). It's then a 90-minute train ride to Verona. The trip from London to Milan takes around 24 hours.

ENTRY FORMALITIES

Citizens of Ireland, USA, Canada, New Zealand and Australia need only a valid passport to enter Italy and do not require visas for stays of up to 90 days. European citizens may stay without a visa for an unlimited period. Citizens of South Africa must have visas to enter Italy.

EU citizens can bring goods for personal use when arriving from another EU country, but must observe the limits on tobacco (800 cigarettes) and spirits (10 litres over 22 per cent alcohol, 90 litres of wine). Limits for non-EU nationals are 200 cigarettes, one litre of spirits and two litres of wine.

MONEY

The euro (€) is the official currency in Italy. There are seven banknotes: €5, €10, €20, €50, €100, €200 and €500. €1 = 100 cents. Coins are in denominations of €1 and €2, and 1, 2, 5, 10, 20 and 50 cents. Currency exchange facilities and ATMs are near the arrival gates at Malpensa, Catullo and Brescia Airports. An ATM is in the rail station in Verona, but it is wise to arrive with some euros, especially at the weekend.

Avoid carrying large amounts of cash and, if you must, hide it well in several concealed pockets and security pouches. Safer are traveller's cheques, accepted at banks and larger hotels, but difficult to cash elsewhere. Both VISA and MasterCard are widely accepted in Italy; American Express is often accepted as well. Many small hotels, *agriturismo* properties and small restaurants do not accept cards. ATMs (*bancomat* in Italian) offer the best exchange rates and are found even in small towns. Ensure that you have enough euros to last over weekends, when banks are closed and ATMs may be out of money or out of order.

HEALTH, SAFETY & CRIME

Verona is considered safe, but as in any large city, be aware of your
surroundings, and avoid walking alone at night or in places that are
not well lit. Guard against pickpockets by carrying only the cash you
need. Waist packs and bum bags label you as a tourist and make you
a potential target anywhere. Wear a shoulder bag across your chest
and keep it fastened closed and in sight at all times. Be especially
wary of crowded areas, such as train stations, buses and street
markets. Avoid groups of children who may try to engage you in
conversation; they are fast and work expertly in teams. Keep cameras
firmly in your hand and the strap around your neck, or better yet,
tucked away, out of sight. Do not leave cameras or handbags slung
over the back of your chair in a restaurant.

Report any thefts immediately, and be sure to get a copy of the police
report (*denuncia*) for insurance. There are different kinds of policemen,
including *carabinieri* (national police) and *vigili* (local officers). Both
are armed and can make arrests, but the *vigili* are usually more
concerned with traffic and parking. You can report a crime to either,
but the paperwork must be completed at a *questura* (police station).

Although tap water is supposedly safe to drink, in many buildings
pipes are old and purification systems haven't been modernised.
It's best to buy bottled water if possible. Pharmacies are abundant
(identified by a green cross outside), but try to carry your favourite
medication for an upset stomach just in case.

Medical care in Italy is very good and emergency treatment at
hospitals is free for everyone who needs it. EU residents carrying
a European Health Insurance Card (EHIC) are entitled to free or
reduced cost non-emergency treatment. UK residents should check
Ⓦ www.ehic.org for more information on getting a card. Non-EU
residents should ensure they have adequate travel and health

insurance in case of any mishaps while abroad. If you have to pay for any treatment upfront, be sure to keep all receipts and prescriptions. In any case, it is advisable to have full travel insurance covering not just medical expenses but theft, loss and cancellation.

Check the following websites for any additional information needed:

Travel & health advice for British citizens Ⓦ www.fco.gov.uk/travel
Ⓦ www.dh.gov.uk/travellers

Travel & health advice for American citizens Ⓦ www.cdc.gov/travel,
Ⓦ www.healthfinder.com

World Health Organisation Ⓦ www.who.int

For police and medical emergency numbers, see Emergencies, page 152.

As a pedestrian, always look both ways when crossing, even on one-way streets, since bus lanes sometimes travel in the opposite direction. Those from left-hand drive countries need to be especially careful because traffic will be approaching from an unexpected direction. Scooters and motorbikes are very common, and you should always be aware of these approaching between vehicles or emerging suddenly from alleyways.

OPENING HOURS

Most of Verona's major attractions and museums are open 08.30 or 09.00–19.00 or 19.30 with Monday morning closing. Smaller ones and some churches may have shorter hours, frequently closing for lunch. The major churches are open through the day, without lunchtime closing from March to October. Hours are subject to change, so ask at the tourist office for the most up-to-date times (websites can be notoriously out of date). Banks open 08.30–13.00 or 13.30 Mon–Fri, with an additional hour in the afternoon (approximately 15.00–16.00). Larger stores generally open 09.00 or 10.00–19.00 or 19.30 Mon–Sat, smaller ones usually close from 12.30 until 15.30 in the summer, with a shorter midday closing in the winter and Monday morning closing. Sunday afternoon openings are becoming more common. Food shops close on Wednesday afternoons. Street markets open about 07.00 and close around midday. Chemists (pharmacies) are usually open 08.00–13.00 and 16.00–20.00 Mon–Sat, and a sign on the door will direct you to the nearest one open longer hours.

TOILETS

Public buildings, such as museums, usually have clean toilets in the publicly accessible areas near the entrance (or will let you in to use one in an emergency), and you will find public facilities at Piazza Brà (enter from the park, just opposite the Palazzo della Gran Guardia) and near the church of San Zeno. The easiest solution elsewhere is to step into a bar or café and go directly to the back, following the sign 'toilet' or the universal symbols. Err on the side of etiquette and buy a quick coffee at the bar, in exchange for their hospitality. Some of these may not be the cleanest you have ever encountered (always carry your own paper), but they are available. At public toilets, be prepared to pay a small fee, usually €0.50.

CHILDREN

Italians love children and it is becoming more and more common to see them in restaurants, even in the evening – although it's rare in upmarket restaurants. Better to choose a small *trattoria*, where your whole family will be welcomed. Hotels can usually provide cots free of charge (with advance notice), and you will rarely be charged for a child staying in a room with adults. Special infant needs, such as baby food and nappies, are available in supermarkets, but for a shorter stay it is easier to bring familiar brands from home.

The most child-friendly sights in Verona are those left by the

Romans: the Arena (see page 78), Teatro Romano (see page 69) and the Arco dei Gavi (see page 78) – be sure they find the chariot tracks in the stones underneath this one. Kids also like the castellated bridge at Castelvecchio (there is a play park for them at the far end) and the natural history museum (Museo Civico di Storia Naturale, see page 86), where there are lots of fossils. When energy flags, head for one of Verona's many *gelato* (ice cream) counters – there is an especially good one just outside the gate at the end of Piazza Brà.

Lake Garda, the Valpolicella region and other towns close to Verona hold a number of attractions that kids will like, including the obvious theme parks and water amusements, such as the almost overwhelming Gardaland (see page 130). Castles are always good, and you'll find these in Sirmione, Malcesine and Soave. Malcesine also has a revolving cable car to the mountaintop of Monte Baldo. Boat rides on the lake are a diversion, too.

In the lake towns, look for kiddie playgrounds, with slides and climbing jungles, swings and other toys. In Verona you'll find one at the other side of Ponte Scaligero. Each May, Verona has the Mondadori Junior Festival (see page 9), where at weekends kids can learn to make ravioli, meet story-book characters, play on rides and take part in a city-full of other activities.

COMMUNICATIONS
Internet
Most hotels now have in-room points or Wi-Fi, or will provide a cable for you to plug into their phone systems. Tourist information offices and kiosks can provide lists of internet cafés and public access points such as libraries, or head to:

Internet Etc ⓐ Via 4 Spade 3/B ⓣ (045) 8000 222 ⓦ internetetc.it
Be sure to bring your passport, as ID is required by law.

Phone

All Verona numbers begin with 045. Numbers vary between six and nine digits, with a few shorter ones remaining. Numbers beginning with 800 are free to call from inside Italy. To use public telephones, buy a card (*scheda telefonica*) from a *tabacchaio* (tobacconist shop), designated by a white capital T on a black background. Hotel telephones usually carry a high surcharge; check at the desk.

Mobile phone numbers begin with a 3; if you see an old number with the prefix 03, omit the zero. You can purchase an Italian SIM card and airtime for your mobile phone at numerous shops around town. If you intend to use your home mobile phone and SIM card, check with your provider whether you need to activate Roaming. Also check rates of making and receiving calls while abroad.

If you are staying more than a few days, it is generally cheaper to purchase an Italian SIM card instead.

TELEPHONING ITALY

To call Verona from abroad, dial the international dialling code (00 from the UK, 011 from the US), followed by Italy's country code (39), followed by the area code (045) and the local number. Note that in Italy, unlike most countries, you should not drop the initial zero on the area code.

TELEPHONING ABROAD

To make an international call from Italy, dial 00, then the country code (UK 44, Ireland 353, US and Canada 1, Australia 61, New Zealand 64, South Africa 27), area code (omitting the initial zero if there is one) and local number.

Post

The Italian postal service is quite reliable. For letters and postcards you can buy *francobolli* (stamps) at a *tabacchaio* (tobacconist), and for special services you can go to a post office. Post office opening hours are approximately 08.15–13.30 on weekdays and 08.15–12.30 on Saturdays. If you pay extra for *posta priorità* (priority post), your card or letter should arrive the next day in Italy, within three days in the UK and about five days elsewhere.

Post Office 📧 Piazza Viviani & Via Carlo Cattaneo 📞 (045) 800 3998 🌐 www.posteitaliane.it

ELECTRICITY

Electrical current in Italy is 220V AC and plugs are the standard two pin, round-pronged type.

British and US appliances will need a plug adaptor, easily obtained at any electrical or hardware store in Verona or at the airport during your travels.

TRAVELLERS WITH DISABILITIES

Travelling around Italy is becoming easier for people with disabilities, but if possible try to travel with an Italian-speaking companion. Milan's Malpensa Airport is fully accessible, with assistance given through a programme called the Sala Amica. If you are arriving at the smaller Valerio Catullo or Brescia airports (see pages 46 & 47), arrange assistance via your airline well in advance.

Train travel is possible for wheelchair users. Look out for the booklet *I Servizi per la Clientela Disabile* at any rail station, listing the stations with reception centres for people with disabilities (Centro di Accoglienza Disabili). For assistance at Milan's Stazione Centrale, call ℹ (02) 6707 0958. The ticket station and the waiting areas are accessible and the platforms are accessed by lift. All tracks at Verona's rail station have lift access, but special assistance is required for boarding trains at any station. Be sure to allow extra time.

When booking a hotel, ask to speak to an English-speaking manager and make sure your needs are understood. Upper-range hotels are more likely to have good facilities for disabled guests. If possible, get someone in Verona to check the accommodation out for you before arrival.

In addition, useful organisations for advice and information before your travels include:

RADAR The principal UK forum for people with disabilities.
🄰 12 City Forum, 250 City Road, London EC1V 8AF 🄣 (020) 7250 3222
🄦 www.radar.org.uk

SATH (Society for Accessible Travel & Hospitality) advises US-based travellers with disabilities. 🄰 347 Fifth Ave, Suite 605, New York, NY 10016 🄣 (212) 447 7284 🄦 www.sath.org

TOURIST INFORMATION

IAT 🄰 Via degli Alpini 9, off Piazza Brà 🄣 (045) 806 8680
🄦 www.tourism.verona.it 🄛 08.00–18.30 Mon–Sat, 08.30–17.00 Sun
IAT 🄰 Porta Nuova railway station 🄣 (045) 800 0861
🄛 08.00–18.30 Mon–Sat, 08.30–13.00 Sun

For good, current information on the city, visit
🄦 http://portale.comune.verona.it and 🄦 www.italiantourism.com, the Italian national tourism (**Ente Nazionale Italiano per il Turismo**, or **ENIT**) site, which has general information on travel in Italy, as well as regional coverage.

BACKGROUND READING

Agnelli Fiat and the Network of Italian Power by Alan Friedman. An

intriguing account of the attitudes that pervade the Italian psyche.
Italian Neighbours and *A Season with Verona* by Tim Parks. Humorous
(football obsessed) expat accounts of living in Verona.
Romeo & Juliet by William Shakespeare. Wherefore art thou? Thou
art in Verona, so learn a speech and impress your date.

⬥ *Monte Baldo cable car (see page 128)*

Emergencies

The following are emergency free-call numbers:

Ambulance (*Ambulanza*) 🕿 118
Fire (*Vigili del Fuoco*) 🕿 115
Police (*Polizia*, English-speaking helpline) 🕿 112

MEDICAL SERVICES

Should you become ill while travelling, you have several sources
of information on English-speaking doctors. If you can reach your
consulate, it can provide a list, or you can go prepared with the
appropriate pages from the directory published by **IAMAT**. The
International Association of Medical Assistance for Travellers is
a non-profit organisation that provides medical information on
health-related travel issues all over the world, as well as a list of
English-speaking doctors (🆆 www.iamat.org). Hospital accident
and emergency departments (ask for the *pronto soccorso*) are open
24 hours daily and must treat you free of charge in an emergency.
Medical Emergency Dial 🕿 118, a free call to ambulances and
emergency medical care.
Chemists (Pharmacies) Emergency Information 🕿 (045) 801 1148
🆆 www.farmacieverona.it

POLICE

Should you need to report a theft (*furto*), missing person or any
other matter to the police, go to the *questura* (police station).
If insurance is involved, ask for a *denuncia*, a stamped form that
you must have for filing claims.
Questura (Main Police Station) 🄰 Lungadige Galtarossa 11
🕿 (045) 809 0411 🆆 http://questure.poliziadistato.it

Polizia Municipale (City Police) ⓐ Via del Pontiere 32/A
ⓣ (045) 807 8411

ADDITIONAL USEFUL NUMBERS
Breakdown
Members of the Automobile Association in the UK have reciprocal
privileges with the Italian Automobile Association. For roadside
assistance and breakdowns, contact **ACI Breakdown Service** ⓣ 116

Lost or stolen credit cards
American Express ⓣ +44 1273 696 933
Diners Club ⓣ +44 1252 513 500
MasterCard ⓣ 800 870 866
Visa ⓣ 800 819 014 (US and UK cardholders)

Lost property
ⓐ Oggetti Smarriti Via campo Marzo 9 ⓣ (045) 807 9341

EMERGENCY PHRASES

Help!	Fire!	Stop!
Aiuto!	Fuoco!	Fermi!
Ahyootoh!	*Fwohkoh!*	*Fehrmee!*

Call an ambulance/a doctor/the police/the fire service!
Chiami un'ambulanza/un medico/la polizia/i pompieri!
Kyahmee oon ahmboolahntsa/oon mehdeecoh/lah
pohleetseeyah/ee pohmpyehree!

EMBASSIES & CONSULATES

In general, it is a consulate that handles emergencies of travelling citizens, not the embassy. But if there is no consulate in a country, then embassies take over these responsibilities. Your nearest consulate or embassy should be the first place you turn to if a passport is lost, after reporting it to the police. Consulates can also provide lists of English-speaking doctors and dentists and can help you to find an English-speaking lawyer.

Australian Embassy ⓐ Via Antonio Bosio 5, Rome ⓣ (06) 852 721
ⓦ www.italy.embassy.gov.au
British Consulate ⓐ Via San Paolo 7, Milan ⓣ (02) 723 001
ⓦ http://ukinitaly.fco.gov.uk
Canadian Embassy ⓐ Via Zara 30, Rome ⓣ (06) 8544 42911
ⓦ www.italy.gc.ca
Irish Consulate ⓐ Piazza San Pietro in Gessate 2, Milan
ⓣ (02) 5518 7569 ⓦ www.ambasciata-irlanda.it
New Zealand Consulate ⓐ Via Terraggio 17, Milan ⓣ (02) 7217 0001
ⓦ www.nzembassy.com
South African Consulate ⓐ Vicolo San Giovanni sul Muro 4, Milan
ⓣ (02) 885 8581 ⓦ www.sudafrica.it
US Consulate ⓐ Via Principe Amedeo 2/10, Milan ⓣ (02) 290 351
ⓦ http://italy.usembassy.gov

⊙ *Friendly police stroll the city streets*

Editorial/project management: Lisa Plumridge
Copy editor: Monica Guy
Layout/DTP: Alison Rayner

The publishers would like to thank the following individuals and organisations for supplying their copyright photographs for this book: Sante J Achille, page 119; Baglioni Hotels, page 33; Luke Daniek/iStockphoto.com, page 113; Dave Dave/SXC.hu, pages 108–9; Dreamstime.com (Daren Baker, page 155; Uwe Blosfeld, page 111; Rob Bouwman, page 93; Ivonne Wierink, page 102); Nicolas Kopp/Fotolia, page 55; John Rattle/BigStockPhoto.com, pages 38–9; Kathryn Tomasetti, pages 5, 17, 21, 62, 117 & 139; Stillman Rogers, all others.

Send your thoughts to
books@thomascook.com

- Found a great bar, club, shop or must-see sight that we don't feature?
- Like to tip us off about any information that needs a little updating?
- Want to tell us what you love about this handy little guidebook and more importantly how we can make it even handier?

Then here's your chance to tell all! Send us ideas, discoveries and recommendations today and then look out for your valuable input in the next edition of this title.

Email the above address (stating the title) or write to:
pocket guides Series Editor, Thomas Cook Publishing, PO Box 227, Coningsby Road, Peterborough PE3 8SB, UK.

WHAT'S IN YOUR GUIDEBOOK?

Independent authors Impartial up-to-date information from our travel experts who meticulously source local knowledge.

Experience Thomas Cook's 165 years in the travel industry and guidebook publishing enriches every word with expertise you can trust.

Travel know-how Thomas Cook has thousands of staff working around the globe, all living and breathing travel.

Editors Travel-publishing professionals, pulling everything together to craft a perfect blend of words, pictures, maps and design.

You, the traveller We deliver a practical, no-nonsense approach to information, geared to how you really use it.

Useful phrases

English	Italian	Approx pronunciation
BASICS		
Yes	Sì	*See*
No	No	*Noh*
Please	Per favore	*Pehr fahvohreh*
Thank you	Grazie	*Grahtsyeh*
Hello	Buongiorno/Ciao	*Bwonjohrnoh/Chow*
Goodbye	Arrivederci/Ciao	*Ahreevehderchee/Chow*
Excuse me	Scusi	*Skoozee*
Sorry	Mi dispiace	*Mee deespyahcheh*
That's okay	Va bene	*Vah behneh*
I don't speak Italian	Non parlo italiano	*Non pahrloh eetahlyahnoh*
Do you speak English?	Parla inglese?	*Pahrlah eenglehzeh?*
Good morning	Buongiorno	*Bwonjohrnoh*
Good afternoon	Buon pomeriggio	*Bwon pohmehreejoh*
Good evening	Buona sera	*Bwonah sehrah*
Goodnight	Buona notte	*Bwonah nohteh*
My name is ...	Mi chiamo ...	*Mee kyahmoh ...*
NUMBERS		
One	Uno	*Oonoh*
Two	Due	*Dooeh*
Three	Tre	*Treh*
Four	Quattro	*Kwahttroh*
Five	Cinque	*Cheenkweh*
Six	Sei	*Say*
Seven	Sette	*Sehteh*
Eight	Otto	*Ohtoh*
Nine	Nove	*Nohveh*
Ten	Dieci	*Dyehchee*
Twenty	Venti	*Ventee*
Fifty	Cinquanta	*Cheenkwahntah*
One hundred	Cento	*Chentoh*
SIGNS & NOTICES		
Airport	Aeroporto	*Ahehrohpohrtoh*
Railway station	Stazione ferroviaria	*Statsyoneh fehrohveeahreeyah*
Platform	Binario	*Beenahreeyoh*
Smoking/non-smoking	Fumatori/non fumatori	*Foomahtohree/non foomahtohree*
Toilets	Bagni	*Bahnyee*
Ladies/Gentlemen	Signore/Signori	*Seenyoreh/Seenyohree*
Bus/Tram	Autobus/Tram	*Owtohboos/Trahm*